Praise for
All That Really Matters

"Sheila Walsh's maturity as a writer reaches its apogee in *All That Really Matters*. Her maturity as a Christian climbs to new heights in chapter 5. A woman incapable of mere theory and abstraction, she has walked the long, lonely road to Calvary and thereby lays claim not only to credibility but to our hearts as well."
—BRENNAN MANNING, author of *The Ragamuffin Gospel* and *Ruthless Trust*

"Wherever we are on this journey of faith, Sheila Walsh's book helps us grasp the profound and simple truth that Jesus taught: Many things are important, but if we miss *all that really matters* in life, we've missed it all."
—MARY GRAHAM, president of Women of Faith

"In *All That Really Matters*, Sheila Walsh beautifully communicates a simple, yet powerful picture of the Christian life as it was meant to be lived—a growing, sustaining love for Christ and others."
—DR. BILL BRIGHT, founder of Campus Crusade for Christ

"What matters more than enjoying a love that never lets you go? *Nothing!* In this delightful book, my dear friend Sheila Walsh shows us that kind of love—how we can receive it from God and give it to others on a daily basis. I encourage you to read this book and rest in the fact that Jesus' simple plan was designed from the very beginning…with you in mind."
—LUCI SWINDOLL, Women of Faith speaker and
author of *I Married Adventure*

"Whenever I see a woman happily juggling fifteen plates—and hardly dropping a one—I always want to ask, 'How do you do it?' I listen up when she replies, 'All that really matters is…' My friend Sheila is, perhaps, one of the busiest and happiest women I know, but she has found what truly matters (despite one or two broken plates now and then). Listen to her wisdom in this wonderful new book, and your life can't help but be transformed."

—JONI EARECKSON TADA, president of Joni and Friends

"Sheila's pen is full of tenderness as she invites us to journey with her into the heart of God. In these uncertain times this book serves as a candle, helping us distinguish a path in the darkness, and a comfort, helping us settle into God's love—*all that really matters.*"

—PATSY CLAIRMONT, Women of Faith speaker and author of *The Shoe Box*

"Sheila's book reminds me of what I love about our faith. It deals with life as it really is and shows that a very real God is right there all along, no matter what may be happening. She has underlined for us a simple message: 'Deal with reality, whatever it is, with a real God as he truly is—the One who loves you.'"

—HENRY CLOUD, PH.D., psychologist and coauthor of *Boundaries*

"*All That Really Matters* reminded me, yet again, that I am not transformed when I 'get it right.' Quite simply, I'm transformed as I enter into the presence of Jesus and allow him to love me."

—MARILYN MEBERG, Women of Faith speaker and author of *I'd Rather Be Laughing*

"Sheila arouses your appetite for Bible study, tantalizes your memory to reflect on the way it was or the way you thought it was, and propels you to an understanding of your lack of control over others, coming to God as you are, realizing that he is in control, and rejoicing that God will open the eyes of your heart because he loves you unconditionally."

—THELMA WELLS, Women of Faith speaker, president of A Woman of God Ministries, and professor at Master's Divinity School and Graduate School

ALL
THAT
REALLY
MATTERS

ALL
THAT
REALLY
MATTERS

JESUS' SIMPLE PLAN *for a* TRANSFORMED LIFE

SHEILA WALSH

WATERBROOK
PRESS

ALL THAT REALLY MATTERS
PUBLISHED BY WATERBROOK PRESS
2375 Telstar Drive, Suite 160
Colorado Springs, Colorado 80920
A division of Random House, Inc.

ISBN 1-57856-330-5

Published in association with Yates & Yates, LLP, Literary Agent, Orange, California.

Library of Congress Cataloging-in-Publication Data
Walsh, Sheila, 1956-
    All that really matters : Jesus' simple plan for a transformed life / Sheila Walsh.
      p. cm.
    ISBN 1-57856-330-5
    1. God—Worship and love. 2. Christian life. I. Title.
    BV4817.W355 2003
    248.4—dc21

2002155423

Printed in the United States of America
2003

10 9 8 7 6 5 4

In loving memory of my friend Debbie Gibson,

who understood as few do this side of eternity

all that really matters

CONTENTS

ACKNOWLEDGMENTS

I am grateful to the staff at WaterBrook Press, particularly Steve Cobb for his gracious spirit, Laura Barker for her conscientious and loving care, and Mark Ford for his flexibility above and beyond what would seem reasonable.

I am thankful for the careful nurture and passionate commitment of my editor, Traci Mullins. An editor is not called to care so much; it is a gift that you do care.

I am thankful to Sealy Yates and his staff, who bring their wisdom and counsel to my life.

Thank you to Mary Graham and my companions at Women of Faith: Patsy Clairmont, Luci Swindoll, Marilyn Meberg, Thelma Wells, Nicole Johnson, and Lana Bateman. My life is graced with joy because you are my dearest friends.

I am grateful to Roy Carter, senior associate pastor at Christ Presbyterian Church in Nashville, for the sermon that ignited a flame in my heart.

My heart overflows with love for the two men who begin and end each day with me: my husband, Barry, and my son, Christian.

Lord Jesus Christ, your love is changing my life moment by moment. There are no words on earth to thank you for your love, grace, and mercy. The greatest privilege in my life is loving you.

To all who have a hunger to know and love Jesus with passion, I am your grateful traveling companion.

My heart is not proud, O LORD,
my eyes are not haughty;
I do not concern myself with great matters
or things too wonderful for me.

PSALM 131:1

Love is life. All, everything that I understand,
I understand only because I love.

LEO TOLSTOY

"Love the Lord your God with all your heart and with all your soul
and with all your strength and with all your mind";
and, "Love your neighbor as yourself."

LUKE 10:27

CHAPTER ONE

ALL THAT REALLY MATTERS

Embracing Jesus' Simple Plan

Life is so much easier now. We know what to expect, and that is quite a relief as you can imagine. It has taken some time, but with perseverance, dedication, and single-mindedness we have finally arrived at this wonderful, peaceful place. We have God in a box!

Not everyone understands the glorious simplicity of our lives. Some have asked about the struggles of the faithful throughout the centuries, pointing to that heartbreaking passage the writer to the Hebrews felt compelled to include. You can find it in chapter 11, but something that extreme can so easily be taken out of context. Another well-meaning sister pointed to the life of Job and the multitude of his sufferings, but we explained to her, "There had to be some reason that God allowed him to suffer so. After all, you never really know what is going on in someone else's life, do you?"

But the best news is that we have finally found what all the faithful have been searching for through the years: the key to understanding the ways of God. We have a statement of faith of sorts that you might find helpful: If you are sick, God will heal you—that is, if you have enough faith and harbor no unconfessed sin. If you give to God, he gives to you. It never fails. Now we're not talking here only about intangible spiritual gifts such as peace or grace. We mean that God is very practical, too. If you need a house, a car, a better job, a spouse, a child, the stuff that God would want you to have, the stuff that makes life worth living, give to God, and he will give to you. The bottom line is that God wants you to be happy. It's a testimony to the world when they see God's people thrive, don't you agree?

> Then Jesus said to his disciples, "If anyone would come
> after me, he must deny himself and take up his cross
> and follow me." (Matthew 16:24)

I hope I have offended you with my irreverent little tale. Much of it is exaggerated, but there is a kernel of truth in it that prompted my passion for this book. The idea behind the fable is to shake the tree of pop-culture Christianity to see what falls off and what remains. Hopefully what will remain is what it really means to be a disciple of Christ whether we are rich or poor, ten years old or ninety years old, living in Chicago, Illinois, or in Calcutta, India. There is nothing in life that is more important than loving God and letting his love flow through us to others.

I've spent a significant amount of time in the past few years talking and writing about the love of God, about how much God loves you and me. That is gloriously true. It has changed my life and continues to change it every day. I believe that if we grasped even a fragment of the truth of this holy love, we would hardly be able to stand in God's presence. His love is overwhelming.

In this book, however, I want to look more closely at what it means for us to love God, for us to commit to passionately pursue God for who he is with all we have and all we are. Jesus left a simple plan for us. It's an uncomplicated plan but one that will transform our lives if we embrace it.

JESUS' SIMPLE PLAN

During the three years of Jesus' ministry on earth, he was either being hounded by crowds of people who were longing for a sign that God was with them—a miracle, a healing—or he was being attacked by religious groups that were offended by his influence. We often group the two primary Jewish sects of Jesus' day, the Pharisees and Sadducees, together, but they were very different in their theology. The Sadducees were a faction of skeptics, determined to trap Jesus and cause him to stumble over his own words. They came up with all sorts of unlikely scenarios, twisted plots, and questions of the Law, always hoping to publicly ridicule and discredit him. This powerful, elitist group was not popular with the masses, but they exerted great influence, both in politics and religion. Their group was comprised of the urban, wealthy, sophisticated class, and they were centered in Jerusalem. The high priest was usually chosen from their ranks. Interestingly, after Jerusalem was destroyed in A.D. 70, they disappeared from history and were never heard from again.

Mark, in his gospel, described the Sadducees as those who didn't believe in a resurrection. For them the whole canon of Scripture was the Pentateuch, the first five books of the Bible. As far as they were concerned, if Moses didn't spell it out clearly, they placed no credence in it. This set them at odds with the Pharisees, who considered the oral tradition, the Word of God passed on from generation to generation, as authoritative as the written Scriptures.

The Sadducees' question to Jesus on one particular day was intended to show how ridiculous the concept of resurrection was and the potential problems it would present. The text they quoted from was Deuteronomy 25:5: "If brothers are living together and one of them dies without a son, his widow must not marry outside the family. Her husband's brother shall take her and marry her and fulfill the duty of a brother-in-law to her."

The Sadducees thought they were brilliantly challenging Jesus by asking what would happen if a man had seven brothers. He married and died without children, so the next brother married her. He, too, died before they had children, so the next brother married her, and on and on. Finally the woman died. At the resurrection whose wife would she be? they asked.

Jesus answered that at the resurrection there will be a whole new way of living. We won't marry or be tied down to any earthly longing, for we will be in God's presence forever, like the angels—complete, gloriously alive, and perfect. Jesus then went on to quote from the very books the Sadducees stood on as their bully pulpit to expose their ignorance of the content of Moses' message. "Now about the dead rising," Jesus said, "have you not read in the book of Moses, in the account of the bush, how God said to him, 'I am the God of Abraham, the God of Isaac, and the God of Jacob'? He is not the God of the dead, but of the living. You are badly mistaken!" (Mark 12:26-27).

This passage was one of the most sacred to the Sadducees, and yet they had missed the point. When God addressed Moses, he said, I *am* the God of Abraham, the God of Isaac, and the God of Jacob—not I *was,* but I *am.* When Moses met God at the burning bush, Abraham, Isaac, and Jacob had been dead for some time. As you can imagine, the Sadducees were furious that Jesus outwitted them by using words from the very books they treasured!

There was a teacher of the Law in the crowd who had slipped in as this debate was going on. He was impressed with Jesus' knowledge of the Law, so he asked him a question of his own. "Of all the commandments, which is the most important?" (Mark 12:28). That might seem like a simple question to us, but it's important to remember that the Jewish rabbis counted 613 individual statutes in the Law. There were 365 laws concerning things you shouldn't do and 248 rules you should obey. To guard against breaking the third commandment, "Do not take the name of the Lord in vain," the religious leaders simply refused to say God's name at all. To save themselves from the lure of adultery, they wouldn't look at women. The most extreme Pharisees earned the title "bleeding Pharisees" because in their manic avoidance of women, they would stare at the ground and often walked into walls and each other!

There was an ongoing debate as to which commandments were the great ones and which ones were the lesser. In that context the rabbi's question was a very important one. How do we plow through 613 statutes and find the one that is the most important? Is it even possible? Jesus says it is.

> "The most important one," answered Jesus, "is this: 'Hear, O Israel, the Lord our God, the Lord is one. Love the Lord your God with all your heart and with all your soul and with all your mind and with all your strength.' The second is this: 'Love your neighbor as yourself.' There is no commandment greater than these." (Mark 12:29-31)

Wow! the rabbi might have thought. *Two, and I just asked for one.* The truth is that they are one. Even though Jesus quoted them from two different places in the Pentateuch (Deuteronomy 6:4-5 and Leviticus 19:18), they are inseparable. From our vantage point in history, perhaps it's easy to pull out what would be most important, but think what it must have been like for the crowd that day. They were drowning in a sea of dos and don'ts, and Jesus told them clearly that all that really matters is to love God with all you have and are and to love your neighbor as yourself.

The rabbi replied, "You are right in saying that God is one and there is no other but him. To love him with all your heart, with all your understanding and with all your strength, and to love your neighbor as yourself is more important than all burnt offerings and sacrifices." When Jesus heard this man answer so wisely, he told him that he was not far from the kingdom of God (Mark 12:32-34).

That's it! That's all that really matters. Love God with all you have and are, and love others as yourself. It is a simple plan but a profound one. It is revolutionary. Perhaps it sounds *too* simple. It might seem easier to make our own list of rules and regulations because that would make us feel as if we were in control. If we could just fill our boxes with what we think it looks like to be good Christians, then we would be safe. But God will not live in a box, and the wonderful news is that he doesn't want you or me to live in a box either.

A RELATIONSHIP WITH GOD

My friend Luci Swindoll tells a story about an interesting encounter she had as she was hurrying home to watch a favorite television show. As a self-confessed meticulous guardian of her private time, she was intent in her pursuit. As she left an optician's office where she'd had an appointment, she heard a faint cry for help. What to do? Should she hurry on by, assuming that someone with more time on his or her hands would soon pass?

She decided to stop and discovered that the source of the cry was an elderly lady; I'll call her Mary. She was lying on the road behind the back tire of a truck. Mary had fallen off the sidewalk and was in some pain. Another onlooker called 911 as Luci sat with the injured woman. When the ambulance arrived, Mary asked Luci to take her purse and follow the ambulance in her car so that she could be with her at the hospital. Luci looked at her watch, sighed, and like the Good Samaritan she is, she added her vehicle to the flashing convoy.

After Luci had spent some time in the waiting room, a nurse told her that Mary had asked for her. Luci went into her room and sat with her for a while. Not knowing the extent of her injuries and wondering if Mary knew Jesus, Luci broached the subject. "Mary, do you have a relationship with God?"

Mary looked at Luci with passionate conviction and replied, "Oh yes! I've read all the magazines."

That was an unexpected answer, and I laughed when Luci told me, but in retrospect I wonder if Mary's answer is all that different from the one we might give.

"Do you have a relationship with God?"

Oh yes! I go to church twice every Sunday.

I'm on my third read through the whole Bible.

I've read everything that Max Lucado and Billy Graham ever wrote.

I'm in a small group.

I tithe 10 percent...sometimes more!

I don't drink, don't smoke, and don't go to R-rated movies. See, I have
a list!

But that's not how Jesus defined a life in relationship with God.

> "Love the Lord your God with all your heart and with
> all your soul and with all your strength and with all
> your mind"; and, "Love your neighbor as yourself."
> (Luke 10:27)

This is all that really matters.

"WHERE'S THE KEY?"

It's Wednesday morning, and I have one free day to write, pick up the dry cleaning, and run forty other errands before I have to get back on the road. I'm hurrying through a department store in the mall when one of the girls behind a cosmetic counter calls out to me. I assume she has decided that I am in need of a makeover, she has the technology, and she can rebuild me.

"I read one of your books," she begins. "Where's the key?"

"The key to what?" I ask, a little confused, wondering if she thinks I ran off with the key to the ladies' rest room.

"The key to knowing how to unlock everything God has for you.

I need a breakthrough. I know God has put things in me, but how do I get to the place where I can use them?"

"You're there," I answered.

"What do you mean?" she asked.

"Let me ask you a question," I replied. "What does it look like to be in relationship with God through Jesus Christ?"

"Well…it means you are doing things for God, being used by him, being a witness."

That's not how Jesus defined a life in relationship with God.

That's not what Jesus prayed for you and for me. In his great high priestly prayer recorded in John's gospel, Jesus prayed first for his disciples and followers who were on the earth at that moment, but then he looked down the passage of years to where you and I sit today, and he prayed for us:

> My prayer is not for them alone. I pray also for those who will believe in me through their message, that all of them may be one, Father, just as you are in me and I am in you. May they also be in us so that the world may believe that you have sent me. I have given them the glory that you gave me, that they may be one as we are one: I in them and you in me. May they be brought to complete unity to let the world know that you sent me and have loved them even as you have loved me. (John 17:20-23)

NOT A PERFORMANCE

Women of Faith is where I have found my niche in this world. I am part of a team of five speakers who travel across America and sponsor conferences for women in large arenas. We have about twenty-eight events a year and ten- to twenty-five thousand women attend each one.

We are in our sixth year together, and more than one and a half million women have been part of our Women of Faith events.

I was at a Women of Faith Friday Intensive in the early summer of 2002, a time set aside before the main conference begins for those who want a more in-depth study experience. We meet from nine in the morning until three in the afternoon. My talk that morning was on anger and forgiveness. I talked about teaching Christian, my five-year-old son, how to handle anger. He had shown signs of something boiling just below the surface of his sun-kissed hair. He told me that he thought life was unfair. I agreed. He said he didn't understand why God let bad things happen. (He had already lost two people very dear to him.) I empathized. I told Christian that it is perfectly all right and appropriate to be angry sometimes but you can't hurt yourself and you can't hurt anyone else. We looked at other alternatives and settled on a punching bag and boxing gloves.

As I shared that little slice of family life, a few women laughed while others took notes. Three days later I received an e-mail from a woman who had been at the seminar. She wrote that she had struggled to help her ten-year-old son deal with what he felt about her divorce from his father. "I made him think he had to stuff it and be a good, strong boy because we are a Christian family. When I got back after the conference, I told him that it was perfectly all right to be angry and that God would love him just as much and so would his daddy and I. My son threw himself into my arms and cried pent-up tears of relief that he could be himself and still be loved by God."

Where did we get the idea that a relationship with God is a performance?

Mary Graham, president of Women of Faith, had met with the speaker team on Thursday night before the conference began on Friday.

"The arena has double-booked," she told us.

"Double-booked?" Patsy Clairmont said in amazement. "We have fifteen thousand women coming tomorrow night. Who are we double-booked with?"

"A dog show," Mary quietly replied, anticipating the outburst of inevitable one-liners she knew would pour forth from the five of us who make up the team.

"Keep your kennel area clean," Luci admonished.

"I start my grooming at five o'clock sharp," Marilyn Meberg added.

Our banter went on for some time. We laughed and laughed. When we settled down enough for Mary to talk over our quips, she told us that the dog show would be in the smaller arena beneath us but our book tables would have to be in the same area. We loved that! Before the conference began, I walked through the grooming area, checking out the variety of pooches.

I watched as a desperately focused handler worked with a little terrier. "Can you see the prize? Can you see? See it in your mind! You want it, don't you?"

The little dog looked as if he was about to faint or self-combust under the pressure. I ventured over. "That's a lot of responsibility for a little dog, don't you think?" I suggested, ignoring the inner voice to mind my own business.

"This is his one chance," she replied. "He has two minutes in the ring, and if he blows it, it's all over for him. He has to keep his tail straight."

I left wondering if I could slip the name of a good therapist to the dog when Helga the trainer wasn't watching. I also remember thinking that it's such a relief we don't have to perform for God. If we let our tail drop in the ring, we are not voted out of life.

Then I thought of all the years I'd spent doing just that: performing, craving approval, executing clever feats so that God would give me the blue ribbon. Then I began to discover another way to live. It's a way based on nothing that I bring to the show but based absolutely on what Jesus Christ has already done. My journey and quest to live an honest, real life has taken me through the dark night of clinical depression. For others it's a death, a divorce, or the events of September 11, 2001, that make us say...

There has to be more than this.

Is this what Jesus meant when he talked about an abundant life?

I'm tired of performing. I want to live.

HOW TO LIVE

"I'm so confused," confessed the woman who brought her cup of coffee over to my table in one of my favorite haunts. "I've been told so many different things about what a Christian should look like. One church told me to grow my hair, another to lengthen my skirt. One said makeup was of the devil, and in another they wore so much makeup it was hard to see the person. I've had it. I quit!"

Have you ever felt that way? I have. We have made being in relationship with God so complicated in our diverse religious culture. Jesus made it simple.

As I'm writing this book, I'm in the midst of the busiest time in the Women of Faith conference schedule. We are traveling every weekend, so I write on Mondays, Tuesdays, and Wednesdays. In the early fall of 2002 we had an event in Hartford, Connecticut. It was our second year there, and it was sold out with more than seventeen thousand women. I always go to my book table at each break to sign books and listen to women who want to share their stories or simply say out loud the thoughts and fears that haunt them. Even though the lines are long and time is limited, I've made a commitment to listen only to the one who is standing in front of me, to look in her eyes and not be distracted by the crowd. That's very important to me. So many people feel as if they don't matter, as if no one notices them. How can we expect people to trust that God is always there and always listens if those who come in his name don't?

In that context I don't usually notice anyone until she is next in line. It was the lunch break on Saturday, and I had a long line of women who wanted to get their books signed before Ce Ce Winans took the stage. I looked up at the next in line and saw a familiar face I hadn't seen in ten years. We were patients together in the psych unit in the fall of 1992. She looked at me as if to say, "Do you remember me?" I threw my arms around her, and we both laughed at the gift of this moment.

I remember the first time we met. She came into the hospital a few days after I did. She was very quiet and reserved. She had been a missionary for several years and had experienced a breakdown on the mission field. For a number of days she sat in our group therapy sessions and said nothing. Then one day, out of the blue, she picked up her metal chair, threw it at the wall, and collapsed in a sobbing heap on the floor. We gathered around her and held her for a while. Finally her story began to flow out of the deep, stagnant well inside her soul.

As a child she had been raped by a family member, and the shame and guilt she felt drove her as a young adult to the mission field. It was her way of telling God that she was sorry for what she had done. Unable in her mind to separate herself from the sin of another acted out on the innocent canvas of her life, she carried this load with her everywhere she went. Inside she was desolate. She persevered for as long as she could until finally, by God's mercy, she fell apart and found herself in a place where she could yell and scream and cry at the bitter betrayal of her childhood.

It was a wonderful thing to watch God work in her life over the next two weeks before I was discharged. I watched as she started to smile, and she seemed as surprised as any of us to hear her own laughter. I wondered how long it had been since she had really laughed. After I left the hospital, I lost touch with her, but here she was now, standing in front of me and grinning from ear to ear.

"What are you doing here?" I asked. "Do you live in this area now?"

"No," she replied. "I'm home visiting family. I'm back on the mission field, but this time I'm there because I want to be. I love it!"

We stole a few moments to give each other the shorthand version of the past ten years, but it was her countenance that I won't forget for a long time. She was ten years older and looked twenty years younger. There was brightness in her eyes and softness in her smile. I saw the difference between someone trying to live according to the law and someone living by the grace of God, when the heart is engaged in the venture, not just the will.

I know what that kind of determination feels like. It is based on fear, not love. I remember the anxiety of serving God and hoping he would approve of me. I remember throwing myself into Christian work, volunteering for everything and then resenting being taken for granted. It's a vicious, destructive cycle. When I ended up in the hospital, I was surprised to discover that so many of the other patients were also involved in what we refer to as full-time Christian ministry. They, too, had been grounded by the weight of their religious baggage. Jesus made it so simple; we make it so complicated.

I'm an ardent people watcher, especially in airports. When I see someone struggle under the weight of too much luggage, a bag hanging from every available limb, I remember what that used to feel like spiritually. Jesus invited us to drop our bags and take up the manageable one he has packed especially for us.

As you look at your life today—your relationships, your work, church service, or other arenas that demand your time and energy— are you engaged at every level of your being, or are you on automatic pilot? Jesus said, "I have come that they may have life, and have it to the full" (John 10:10). Does that sound too good to be true? If Jesus said it, it must be true. It's not just the title of a self-help book; it's a promise from the Lamb of God.

I believe that Jesus wants to teach us how to live. If you are tired of jumping through hoops, this book is for you. If you, like me, want to be set free from needing and expecting things from life that we are not promised in the Word of God, then we will journey on together here. If you, like me, passionately desire to live a life that honors God, then let's explore what it means to love him and to love others freely, openly, and wholeheartedly.

How do we do it? Let's begin!

Love the LORD your God with all your heart
and with all your soul and with all your strength.
These commandments that I give you today
are to be upon your hearts.
Impress them on your children.
Talk about them when you sit at home
and when you walk along the road,
when you lie down and when you get up.
Tie them as symbols on your hands
and bind them on your foreheads.
Write them on the doorframes
of your houses and on your gates.

DEUTERONOMY 6:5-9

The charge to Peter was feed my sheep;
not try experiments on my rats.

C. S. LEWIS

Blessed are those who hunger and thirst for righteousness,
for they will be filled.

MATTHEW 5:6

CHAPTER TWO

THE GREAT HUNGER

Yearning for More

If you ever decide to dive into the sea of words and write a book, you will have to face this question: Where do I begin?

I usually look for a springboard that will launch me deep into the storm of thoughts, feelings, and prayers that have been washing back and forth, back and forth for weeks and months in my heart and soul. I rarely write out of what I know. I usually write out of what I long to know. My writing becomes my spiritual journal, and so too with this undertaking.

Rather than one huge leap into the waves with this book, it seems there have been several small squalls that have stirred up the message within my heart. Some of these squalls have shown me my hunger for God and others my squelching of that hunger—my vain attempts to satisfy it with something else.

SQUALL NUMBER ONE: THE GREATEST SIN

One Sunday morning in the early summer of 2002, Roy Carter, senior associate pastor at the church we belong to, preached the first in a series of sermons on loving God. I know that during my forty-six years on this earth I have heard hundreds of sermons on that subject, but that morning it was as fresh as if I had never heard of such an idea. He asked the congregation this question: "What is the greatest sin?"

I'm sure there was a multitude of answers swimming through the air that morning depending on the history, personal background, and spiritual agenda of each person present.

Murder

Adultery

Homosexuality

Blasphemy

Child abuse

Witchcraft

Roy gave us a moment for personal reflection and then announced his answer.

"The greatest sin is not loving God."

There was an audible corporate, "Oh!" The answer seemed so simple, but as with all things that seem simple initially, the answer is proving to be a deep well with fresher water the deeper I go. Roy's message began something in me that continues to this day. I bought the tape of the sermon and listened to it again. I had my own questions:

What does this mean, Lord?

What does it look like to love you with all my heart, soul, mind, and strength? Where do I begin?

I knew deep within my spirit that God was speaking to me, profoundly and lovingly, calling me to a deeper relationship with him. I can trace similar turning points through the years.

I have been on speaking terms with God since I was ten years old. One of my first memories of hearing the voice of God internally was in a small Baptist church on the west coast of Scotland. It wasn't the church we attended, but it was just down the road from where I lived. The youth pastor of our church, Ayr Baptist, told us that New Prestwick Baptist would be showing a movie on the life and death of Christ, and we were invited to go. I signed up. I must have been about thirteen or fourteen at the time. I sat with my girlfriends in the front row, and together we took stock of the crowd, giggling as we surveyed the fleet of boys that made up our sister church's youth group. We all decided that they had a better bunch than our meager offering. Our group was comprised of a large posse of girls and three or four boys.

My mind was not on spiritual pursuits that evening. My girlish agenda was innocent, but as the evening progressed, I knew that God had a different agenda than mine. I don't remember how the movie began or how long it was, but I will never forget the impact that the crucifixion scene had on me. I knew the story well as I was raised in a Christian home and had been immersed in church activities since I was a child. But my spirit had never been arrested this way before.

> It was the third hour when they crucified him. The written notice of the charge against him read: THE KING OF THE JEWS. They crucified two robbers with him, one on his right and one on his left. Those who passed by hurled insults at him, shaking their heads and saying, "So! You who are going to destroy the temple and build it in three days, come down from the cross and save yourself!" (Mark 15:25-30)

Tears poured down my face. It was as if there was no one else in the room, just a dying Jesus and me. I had asked Christ to take control of my life when I was eleven, but I had never had this radical an encounter with the crucified Christ. I had been pulled back through time, and I stood there at the foot of that barbarous tree on Golgotha, the hill shaped for nightmares. Jesus was looking right at me. His eyes were so full of love I could hardly bear it. I wanted to look away but couldn't. I saw what he was doing and had no doubt it was for me.

That encounter changed my perspective on my life. It was no longer possible to carry on with business as usual. Encounters with Christ demand a response. That night I made a vow to love Jesus and to live for him in a way that was new, uncharted territory for me. I walked home with my heart full. As I lay in bed, my sister, Frances, fast asleep beside me, I brought all that I knew to be me to the foot of that cross and laid it at Jesus' feet.

The next few years were filled with Christ-centered activity and evangelism.

When I graduated from high school at eighteen, I had no clear sense of direction. Encounters with Christ are not commonplace. I worked for the local authority in my town for a year, training to be a social worker. But every day was a frustration as human lives were obscured by reams of paperwork. Then I applied to London Bible College, was accepted, and began to train for whatever the next step might be. I had no clear call other than a passionate desire to serve God. When I graduated, I worked as a youth evangelist with British Youth for Christ. It took me many years and many tears, however, before I began to grasp how impossible a task we create for ourselves when our goal is to "do something for God." Jesus said, "It is finished" (John 19:30).

But even as the heady emotions of a committed teenager slipped into the back pages of the journal of my life, my ongoing conversation with God deepened through the years. Great joys, like becoming a mother for the first time at age forty, and aching sadness, like falling into the dark foreboding well of clinical depression in my midthirties, have served to deepen the roots of my faith. I have experienced God in the joy, but as C. S. Lewis observed, pain is like God's megaphone: His voice is clear and steady when life is not.

At the time I heard my pastor's sermon that summer morning last year, I had been involved in Christian ministry for more than twenty years. Suddenly I wondered how much of my life had been wrongly focused. I have a good marriage. I love being a mother with all the joys and frustrations that brings. I am very fulfilled in my work. But I felt as if something was missing. It's not that I was just going through the motions, but there was a persuasive voice deep inside that told me, *There is more.*

I remember sitting out in my yard later that day and taking stock of my life and faith. I imagined being interviewed by Barbara Walters.

"So you believe that you have a relationship with the God of the universe?" she began.

"I do," I replied passionately. "I believe that the same God who turned his head one way and created the sun, then another way and created the moon loves me, and I talk to him every day. He is my life."

"If that is true, how does that perspective affect every moment of your life? It must change everything."

"It does," I replied a little uneasy in my seat. "It certainly should."

But does it? My life is taken up with all sorts of things: laundry, taking Christian to school, speaking and writing and singing, making dinner, feeding the cat and his plethora of buddies…stuff. It's do, do, do and go, go, go. I feel as if I've just begun a day, and I look at the clock, and it's ten at night.

I wonder how much energy I have spent on external "doing" and searching rather than on internal "being" and abiding in God's transforming presence. It's been my desire for years to communicate to others that they are deeply loved by God, but in my own soul I have continued to feel compelled to do the right things as opposed to simply seek God's face. I like to keep all the plates spinning at the same time. When they're in sync, I feel as if I'm doing well. When one or two smash on the ground, I feel I've failed. I sincerely desire to know and love God, but too often I have allowed the busyness of life and my comfort with things more tangible than prayer and silent waiting before God to fill my days. I am encouraged when others tell me that my books or talks or music have brought them closer to God, but when I look in the mirror, I see someone who knows God is there, loves him, takes great comfort in his guidance and the assurance of an eternal relationship, yet has made her life very complicated.

When I was a little girl, I decided that I would be a nun. Our house overlooked a Catholic church, and the priest and his housekeeper were very kind to my sister and me. When the little girls would dress up like brides for their confirmation, they would let us watch from the balcony. It was a breathtaking sight for a romantically motivated child. Then I saw a movie about a nun who gave up everything for God; nothing was too much to sacrifice for him. That was it! It was sealed as if in blood in my soul. I would give up everything that this world had to offer and concentrate on God. Would that life were like that. I have since learned from others that life as a priest or nun is just as challenging as life as a mom or a midwife. So if the job description isn't the problem, then what is?

I have discovered that this quandary is not peculiar to me. There is a soft groan throughout the church that you have to be quiet to hear, but it's there. It's a cry for more—not more stuff, because that has almost choked the life out of us, but a hunger for God. As Augustine said, "Our hearts are restless till they rest in Thee." I used to interpret those famous words as the God-shaped vacuum that exists in those who have no relationship with God, but it's much more. It's a drumming of our fingers on our souls, wondering when we'll get the point.

My son loves to tell jokes. When he sticks with those he has heard from others, he is usually on to a winner, but he loves to branch out. He'll ask, "What do you get when you cross an elephant with a brush? A brushephant!" He waits for the ensuing raucous laughter. If he tells it to Barry or me, he's usually rewarded, but if he tells it to other people, they look at him with a vacant expression, waiting for a punch line that makes sense. I've seen it in their eyes.

That didn't make any sense.

That's not where I thought he was going.

Am I the only one who doesn't get it?

Did I miss the point?

I've seen that same look in the eyes of hundreds of people as they run over the opening lines of their spiritual lives.

Am I missing something here?

Why do I feel so dissatisfied?

Is this all there is?

SQUALL NUMBER TWO: THE OBSCENITY OF DEATH

It was June 2002. For the first time, a Women of Faith conference was being held in Charleston, South Carolina, the birthplace of my husband, Barry. My in-laws, Eleanor and William, had prayed for the conference to be held there, but neither lived to see their prayers realized. The last time we had been in Charleston was to bury William on a cold November day in 2000, just a year and a half after we had buried Eleanor.

Usually Barry, Christian, his nanny, and I arrive in a city on Thursday evening to prepare for the conference, but because it was Charleston and full of memories for us as a family, we flew in on Wednesday morning. Christian's number-one priority was the beach. So we rented a car, checked into our hotel, and with swimsuits, beachball, inflatable alligator, bucket, and spade in tow we drove to Folly Beach on James Island, where Barry lived until he went to college.

Charleston has an aroma all its own. The tall sweet grass sways in the breeze, mingling with the salty air and pungent flowers that, coaxed by the rampant humidity, give off their perfume in overwhelming intensity. Sitting on the beach, I looked over at the pier, remembering an evening when William, Eleanor, Barry, Christian, and I had walked that pier as the sun began to set. William regaled us with tales of catching soft-shell crabs with Barry when he was a boy. They would take them home, and William would cook them with just the right blend of seasonings. I remembered that Eleanor had tied a scarf around her head, as she had just had her hair set and the warm wind and humid air promised to undo what had been carefully done.

A moment. A memory. Then I was pulled back to the present as Christian wanted to stand in the ocean with his back to the waves, an endeavor requiring the presence of one or preferably both parents.

As the sun began to set, we packed up our sandy selves and headed out. Barry pulled over at a small fruit-and-vegetable stand by the side of the highway. He came back with two pounds of boiled peanuts, a Charleston tradition and delicacy. The first time I tried them I hated them. They are large green peanuts, still in their shells, that have been boiled for hours in salty water. Now I had succumbed to their charm. We sat in the car and ate peanuts, windows rolled down, discarded shells everywhere, salty water dripping off our chins onto sandy legs. Bliss!

We dried off as best we could and drove to Holy Cross cemetery, the final resting place of Barry's parents. Christian stayed in the car with his nanny as Barry and I stood under the large oak tree that sheltered their headstone. The comforting words of the psalmist came to my mind: "Find rest, O my soul, in God alone; my hope comes from him" (Psalm 62:5). We stood in silence for some time accompanied by our private memories. I remembered the feeling I'd had as Eleanor's casket was being lowered into the ground—a moment of childlike panic, a feeling of intense claustrophobia pressing in on me. My adult self knew that what was in the casket was just the castoff shell of the woman who had lost her battle with liver cancer, but a small part of me was still plagued by old demons from my father's death when I was four years old and felt horror at the thought of being buried.

We got back in the car and drove to the house where Barry had lived throughout his childhood and where William and Eleanor had lived for forty years. Now the flower beds were overgrown, and the grass looked parched and unloved. William had been an ardent gardener. He had been featured on the local news and had a video clip of the story that he would proudly play over and over again when Barry and I visited.

"Dad would have a fit," Barry said.

I turned to look at Christian, sitting in the backseat of the car, his head resting on the inflatable alligator. I wondered if he would remember this place and what his memories of his grandparents would be. I thought of the morning when hospice care came to remove Eleanor's hospital bed from our house and retrieve the remaining morphine.

Christian, then three, wanted to sit in the room while they dismantled it. As they carried the last piece out, he said, "Nana doesn't need it now. She is in heaven."

"Best place to be, son," the kind man had replied.

Christian didn't seem to remember. Salty tiredness was overtaking him. We drove back to the hotel, and after a hot bath, he and Barry fell fast asleep.

I couldn't sleep. Too many memories vied for a position on center stage. Not wanting to wake Barry or Christian, I sat in the corner of the room with a book and my travel reading light. At about two in the morning I heard a noise. It was Barry weeping into his pillow. I had wondered when the sadness would spill out.

"I hate this," he said as I sat on the edge of the bed and held his hand. "There is something so obscene about death, the whole dying process."

"I know," I agreed, thinking of cancer's relentless takeover of Eleanor's body.

"I think of how she lived," he continued. "All her life she went faithfully to church, but her life was such a struggle with rights and wrongs, rules and regulations, and worry, worry, worry."

I remembered all too well her quest for peace in this world. Giving to television ministries, seeking prayer, longing for healing, wishing she could find the key that would unlock God's heart toward her and change her life. "I don't want to die," she had told me. "Christian will forget me. I don't want to die."

Finally Barry fell asleep, and I sat for a while thinking about our conversation.

Why do we struggle so much?

Why is it so hard to find peace?

What is the ultimate purpose of our lives here on earth?

What is true and real about our faith, and what is simply wishful thinking?

The woman in the department store who was looking for some mystical answer stood shoulder to shoulder with Eleanor in a frustrating attempt to find the key that would unlock heaven and give her what she wanted. But God can't be contained in a book or a conference or promises made by television evangelists. Instead he has given us a simple plan, a different way to live, a narrow path that leads to him and home.

I tell my young son every day, "All you have to do, darling, is love God with all you have and let God love others through you. You don't have to fix anyone, you don't have to be first in your class, and you don't have to win the race. Just love God."

He looks at me with a barely disguised expression that says, "I would rather be first. I would rather win the race."

Why? Is it because it's easier? Because it makes us feel in control?

SQUALL NUMBER THREE: THE DREAM HOUSE

William, Barry, and I sat around the kitchen table. It was covered with papers and pens, brochures and bank statements. Christian was playing on the floor, stuffing large pieces of a jigsaw puzzle into my suede boots.

"What I'd like to do," William began, "is sell the house in Charleston so we could buy a bigger place together."

"Why don't you hold on to your house for a while, Pop?" I said. "You have a lifetime of memories soaked into those walls."

"No, I think it's time," he said. "Will there ever be a time when you won't want me to live with you?"

"Of course not!" Barry and I said in unison. "You are our family," I added. "We are four now, and we like it that way."

"Then I want to sell. You can sell this house, and we can find one with more room. You need an office, Barry, and so does Sheila."

I had to admit that having a place where I could spread out my papers and books without having to move them to set the table for dinner was appealing. I had lost more than one day's work as an eager three-year-old shared his juice with my writing or the cat rolled around on it, sending papers to all corners of the kitchen. It was decided. William put his house on the market, and so did we.

We began to look around at real estate. I hate the process of looking for a new house, but fortunately Barry loves it. Day after day he scoured the highways and byways of Nashville, Tennessee, looking for our dream home. One day he came home and announced that he had found it. He had spent three hours there that afternoon with the Realtor, and he was very excited. It was evening by this time, so William, Christian, and I couldn't get in to see it until the next day.

"Let's just drive by, and I'll show you the outside," Barry suggested, eyes bright with the joy of discovery.

"It's Christian's bedtime, babe," I said.

"I want to see the house! I want to see the house!" Christian chanted, turning his declaration into a march around the kitchen table.

"You just don't want to go to bed, young man," I replied, accepting the inevitability of a late-night trip.

We all bundled into the car. The house was a new one, so no lights were on. Barry stood on tiptoe peering in the windows. He tried the front door.

"You'll get arrested," I warned.

"Isn't it awesome?" Barry replied, refusing to let me rain on his parade.

"Wow, man!" William agreed. "She's a beaut."

"It's lovely," I agreed. "Isn't it a bit too big for us, though?"

"Not if you consider that we need four bedrooms, a decent size office, and some space to avoid bumping into each other," he answered.

The following day we examined every inch and all agreed that it was beautiful. Within no time our house sold, as did William's, so we put an offer on the dream home. After the usual dance of exchanged offers, we settled on a price, signed the contract, and established a move-in date.

It was a lovely home. Christian had a playroom, and I had my own little space to spread out. I immediately declared it a cat-free, juice-free zone. It seemed we were settled, but then life is so unpredictable. Sometimes you get a warning that a squall is ahead. Sometimes it blows up out of nowhere. One November night William went up to take his bath, and within a few moments the canvas of our lives changed forever. He had a heart attack, and in ten minutes he was gone, leaving a discarded shell on the bathroom floor.

We all felt his absence acutely. Barry had now lost both parents, and as an only child, he felt adrift. He and his dad were such good friends, so the vacancy was immense. Christian's grief was fierce. He wept for weeks. I found myself setting the table for four or keeping a part of the newspaper for William to read. Then I would remember, and sadness would sit with me like a gray Scottish winter day. Weeks turned into months, and soon it was a year. The house seemed so big, so empty. We had too much space. Christian wouldn't sleep in his room. It was too far from ours for a five-year-old heart and imagination. I began to wish we could sell the dream house and wondered how Barry would feel about that.

Sometimes the more stuff I have, the farther from God I feel. That's how it was. I began to pray that if we had allowed space and mortgages, furniture and the lure of the so-called American dream too much room in our lives, God would show Barry, too. He did. As I write today, our house is on the market. It's our intention to move into an apartment for a year and then find a smaller house where the building is just a shelter for our lives rather than a show of its own.

I'm not saying that having a big house is wrong or that living in a small space guarantees intimacy or spirituality. What I am saying is that, for me, it's time to find out what occupies a space that only God should live in. There is something powerful and liberating about simplicity.

As Jesus started on his way, a man ran up to him and
fell on his knees before him. "Good teacher," he asked,
"what must I do to inherit eternal life?"

"Why do you call me good?" Jesus answered. "No
one is good—except God alone. You know the commandments: 'Do not murder, do not commit adultery,
do not steal, do not give false testimony, do not
defraud, honor your father and mother.'"

"Teacher," he declared, "all these I have kept since I
was a boy."

Jesus looked at him and loved him. "One thing you
lack," he said. "Go, sell everything you have and give to
the poor, and you will have treasure in heaven. Then
come, follow me." (Mark 10:17-21)

The young man who asked what he had to do to inherit eternal life
had kept all the rules, and yet there was a space inside that rule keeping was not filling. Is it wrong to be rich? I don't think so. I think what
Jesus was saying was not, *What do you have?* but rather, *What has you?*
It's a heart thing and a love issue. Christ longs that we would walk away
from anything that pulls our heart away from him.

SQUALL NUMBER FOUR: THE MOTHER

I met her at a conference. She had waited in my book line for more
than an hour, and now we stood face to face. Her eyes appeared to
carry a weight that dragged down her whole body. I listened.

"We waited for so long to have a child. I never thought it would
happen. Then I discovered I was pregnant. I was overjoyed. Our son
was born two years ago. He's perfect."

I smiled with the understanding of a mother of another perfect
boy. She continued her story.

"We had a real worry with him when he was just one year old. It looked as if he might be really sick."

She saw an expression in my eyes that prompted a quick resolution. "No, he's not sick. That's not the problem. The problem is, I realized that if God took him, I think I would hate God." She buried her face in her hands and wept. "How could the answer to my prayers be the very thing that threatens to shatter my faith?" she asked. "I feel as if I've made an idol of my son. I don't want to, but how can I change what I feel in my heart? Have I put my son in the place that only God should be?"

How I empathized with her heartache. I, too, have felt that internal war when, like a mother protecting her cub, I have stood toe-to-toe with God.

"The truth is that you don't know how you would respond," I suggested. "God's grace meets our pain toe-to-toe. I, too, have wondered how I would respond if something happened to Christian. I know I would be devastated, but I can't limit God's ability to walk beside me as I walk and to carry me through the places where I can't walk. He's done it before, and I have no reason to second-guess him now."

She looked at me for a few moments, moving miles away from me in her heart, and replied, "I guess I love my boy more than you love yours." With that she turned and left.

I prayed for her that evening. It is a terrible thing to live your life constantly anticipating disaster, certain that should it strike, you would curse God and long to die.

Is it wrong to love our children fiercely, wholeheartedly? I don't think so. But we cross a line when our loyalties pull our hearts away from God rather than closer to him. Is God jealous of your relationship with your child, your spouse, or your career? I believe that these things only become idols, impostors, when they consume our lives, leaving no room for him.

Perhaps, like me, you have harbored a misunderstanding about

God's character and ways. There have been times in my life when I thought that if I surrendered an area to God's control, he would take it away just to see if I loved him "enough." When I was sixteen years old, my mother became very sick. It took the doctors some time to get to the root of the pain that washed over her in sickening waves. Finally they decided to do surgery, as they had discovered that she had a tear at the entrance to her stomach that was allowing acid to leak out and consume healthy tissue. She also had a duodenal ulcer, and her gall bladder was full of stones. On the day of her surgery I felt sick inside, afraid that something would go wrong and I would lose her, too. After school that day I took a bus down to the beach in our small town of Ayr. As I walked along the sand, a battle raged inside me. I wanted to release Mom into God's hands and live in his peace, but I was terrified that if I did, he would take her.

I am convinced today that God is not like that. He is a jealous God, but he is also good and kind and loving. *He is a parent too.*

ALL THAT REALLY MATTERS

How can we love God with all our heart, soul, mind, and strength if we don't know him?

It's not possible. But this is my heart's hunger: to know him, to know him, to know him. I believe it's yours, too, or you wouldn't have picked up this book. So we have to start with our hunger and take a deeper look at all that God has revealed about himself to us. Whatever we miss we will be the poorer for.

If you were to ask one of the twenty-five thousand people who receive my newsletter every week, "Do you know Sheila Walsh?" I'm sure they would say yes. They would know the events of the week, the highlights and prayer requests. They would know the latest antics of my son and the impact of the previous weekend's conference. But there would be much they didn't know. They wouldn't know what I like to eat, what secret fears I harbor, whether Barry and I are rested or weary. That's appropriate. There are things about me better left unsaid, prayerfully placed in the sanctification waiting room. With God, however, everything is different. There are things about him we will never grasp here on earth simply because our human sinful bodies and minds can't take them in. But God has revealed to us a lot about who he is, and if we will invest the energy into meditating about these things daily, we will be changed.

Paul wrote this to the church in Ephesus:

> I keep asking that the God of our Lord Jesus Christ,
> the glorious Father, may give you the Spirit of wisdom
> and revelation, so that you may know him better. I pray
> also that the eyes of your heart may be enlightened in
> order that you may know the hope to which he has
> called you, the riches of his glorious inheritance in the
> saints, and his incomparably great power for us who
> believe. (Ephesians 1:17-19)

That would be my prayer for you and me—that God would open the eyes of our hearts. I acknowledge the hunger for God in my own life. I recognize the impostors that have applied for the position. So this is where I begin. C. S. Lewis, in his masterly work *Mere Christianity*, says this: "Your real new self (which is Christ's and also yours, and yours just because it is His) will not come as long as you are looking for it. It will come when you are looking for him."

That seems to be the perfect next step. Who is this God we are called to love? Our lives are grab bags of ideas that we have stuffed into our souls over the years. Some of them are worth keeping, and some should be trashed. I pray that Christ, by the power of the Holy Spirit, would teach us about our Father and fuel our desire to love God with everything we have and are. This is all that really matters.

For who in the skies above can compare with the LORD?

Who is like the LORD among the heavenly beings?

In the council of the holy ones God is greatly feared;

he is more awesome than all who surround him.

O LORD God Almighty, who is like you?

You are mighty, O LORD, and your faithfulness surrounds you.

PSALM 89:6-8

A man can no more diminish God's glory

by refusing to worship him

than a lunatic can put out the sun

by scribbling the word *darkness* on the walls of his cell.

C. S. LEWIS

The loss of the concept of majesty has come

just when the forces of religion are making dramatic gains

and the Churches are more prosperous than at any time

within the past several hundred years.

But the alarming thing is that our gains are mostly external

and our losses are wholly internal.

A. W. TOZER

CHAPTER THREE

GOD IS IN CONTROL

Resting in His Sovereignty

My friend Patsy Clairmont, part of the Women of Faith speaker team, is the consummate storyteller. Offstage she is diminutive and unassuming. She is five feet tall on a good day, quiet and thoughtful compared to the rest of the team. (We tend toward the more raucous swing of the personality pendulum.) When Patsy gets on stage, however, a transformation takes place. As she walks up the five steps that separate our seats from the stage, something happens in her with each step she takes. By the time she gets to the top, she is Amazonian in stature, energized and animated. She fills the stage and the arena with her presence and holds us all in the palm of her hand. I could listen to Patsy tell the same story thirty times and still laugh as hard at the end as I did at the beginning because of the liveliness and joy that inoculate every word.

As a speaker team we love to share stories of the funny things that have happened to us on the road before we began working together. This is a story Patsy told me…

She had been invited to speak at a women's luncheon. During lunch a lady approached her table and told her that she had been given the privilege of introducing her. The conversation went something like this.

"We're so glad you are here, Patsy! Now, I need a few facts about you before I introduce you. What exactly is your degree in?"

"A degree? Actually, I don't have a degree," Patsy replied.

"Oh!" was the mildly appalled response. "Well, never mind. What honors and awards have you received?"

"That would be…none," Patsy said.

"Oh my!" her ruffled hostess replied. "Do you belong to any clubs? Junior League perhaps?"

"No." Patsy's answers were getting shorter as the woman in front of her was getting taller.

In a last-ditch attempt to save the day, the lady asked, "Well, do you golf?"

"I do not," she replied.

"Then what on earth shall I say?" the woman asked, panic mounting with each horrified breath.

"How about, 'Ladies, would you welcome Patsy Clairmont'?"

As her feverishly perspiring hostess choked out a less than convincing introduction, one thing was very clear: This lady had no idea who Patsy was. If she had, she would have known she was introducing one of the best speakers in the country.

I think we fall into the same perplexed pattern with God: We don't really know who he is. If we did, it would transform every aspect of our lives. We may think we know who he is and what he does, but like Patsy's hostess, we don't have all the right information before us.

Think with me for a moment. If we believed that God is in control of every moment of our lives, would we worry so much? If we believed that nothing, absolutely nothing can happen to us today that hasn't first passed through the sovereign hands of our Father in heaven, would we be so anxious, so afraid? If we embraced the truth that God is our provider, our shepherd, our healer, our peace, our joy, our righteousness, our devoted parent, would we still be searching "out there somewhere" for what God has placed inside us? Would we still have the same compulsion to control others or our circumstances?

In January 1855 a twenty-year-old pastor, Charles Haddon Spurgeon, began his sermon with this assertion: "It has been said by someone, 'the proper study of mankind is man.' I will not oppose the idea, but I believe it is equally true that the proper study of God's elect is God." He went on to say, "Would you lose your sorrow? Would you drown your cares? Then go plunge yourself in the Godhead's deepest sea; be lost in his immensity; and you shall come forth as from a couch of rest, refreshed and invigorated."

What a promise! As we look at our lives today with all the unresolved issues, heartaches, fears, and disappointments, our brother's voice echoes to us through the years...

Would you lose your sorrow?

Would you drown your cares?

Lose yourself in God's immensity.

We are often told that the key to peace is self-knowledge. The quote that Spurgeon used in his sermon offers that thought. "It has been said by someone, 'the proper study of mankind is man.'" He was quoting a familiar philosophy espoused by Alexander Pope. The full quote is, "Know then thyself, presume not God to scan: The proper study of mankind is man."

But if we stop at ourselves, if all we pursue is self-knowledge, we will be on a short and ultimately disappointing trip. If we are created in the image of God, then our hope, our joy, our peace, our purpose, and our future lie in God alone. We are invited to dive together into the sea of all that God has revealed to us about himself through his prophets, his written Word, and through his one and only glorious Son. Even though it's not possible with our limited human understanding to grasp all of who God is—for that would surely make us like him, and we are not—we can study what God has shown us about himself. I have heard numerous sermons and songs about the love of God, but we can't stop there. God is not just love. God is also holy, mysterious, all-knowing, and ever-present, above and beyond any created thing. As we prayerfully consider how to love God with all we have and are, we must begin with God, not with ourselves.

NAME ABOVE ALL NAMES

"Those who know your name will trust in you," the psalmist pro-
claims, "for you, LORD, have never forsaken those who seek you"
(Psalm 9:10). There are many great books written solely on the subject
of the names of God, but in this chapter I want to focus on three that
highlight his sovereignty and majesty:

El Elyon: the God who is in control of all things

Jehovah-tsidkenu: the God who is our righteousness in all things

Adonai: the God who is Lord of all things

Now, before you put the book down, thinking, *If I want a sermon
with funny sounding words, I'll wait till Sunday,* let me assure you that I
am not going to ask you to wade through the Hebrew, Greek, and
Latin of all things pertaining to the knowledge of God. But as I have
hungered to know more about who God is and how he acts, I've discovered that there are treasures hidden in the names of God. Jesus told
us that what really matters is to love God and others, so it makes sense
that the more we know about God, the more we will be able to respond
to him with love.

Before we begin to take a closer look at who God is, I want to recommend three books that have been a source of great encouragement
to me as I have studied the character of God. The first is *Lord, I Want
to Know You* by Kay Arthur. I have tremendous admiration for the
wealth of wisdom that flows out of Kay's diligent mining of the riches
of God's Word. In this book she looks at the names of God and what
they tell us about his all-encompassing greatness.

The second book is a modern Christian classic: *Knowing God* by
J. I. Packer. When I graduated from London Bible College in 1975,
Dr. Packer gave the commencement address. Having studied his writings as part of my degree, I was thrilled to hear him in person. He
seemed like a quiet, unassuming man, but his message was large and

demanding. I was twenty-one years old then, but he left his thumbprint of wisdom and passion on my soul.

Twenty-four years later our paths crossed again. I was attending the Christian Booksellers Convention in New Orleans as a guest of Water-Brook Press. I had written six children's books that they were publishing under the banner of Children of Faith. If you have ever been to a CBA event, you know that it's a sea of booths, faces, new books, gifts, and music, all offered in an overwhelming come-and-get-it smorgasbord. After walking the convention floor for several hours, my feet were barking loudly. I retreated to the WaterBrook suite to grab a cup of coffee and to kick off my shoes for ten minutes.

I was sprawled out in a chair, feet on a coffee table like a marine on leave, when one of the editors announced, "Sheila, I'd like you to meet Dr. Packer." Well, I was out of that chair quicker than a manic shopper on the day after Thanksgiving. But instead of saying all the mature, adult, spiritual things I wanted to say, I blurted out, "I think your books are really cool."

Back in my hotel room later I faced an internal firing squad. "Cool!?! You told Dr. J. I. Packer his books are cool?! How old are you…twelve?!"

He had actually been very sweet, saying, "Thank you so much. I don't think anyone has ever said that to me before." Inside I was thinking, *That's because you don't lecture in kindergartens.*

Knowing God is an amazing book that has sold over one million copies. I love what Elisabeth Elliot says about it: "Here is a theologian who puts the hay where the sheep can reach it—plainly shows us ordinary folks what it means to know God."

One of the things I love most about Dr. Packer's writings is that they inspire worship. We live in an information age, but information is not enough. I have read many good Christian books that simply fill my internal backpack with more knowledge and information, but they don't challenge me to change or show me how that would be possible. When I read his book, I want to get down on my knees and worship God. I try to limit my reading of Christian books now to those that make me want to sing "Hallelujah, what a Savior!"

The third book is *The Knowledge of the Holy* by A. W. Tozer. When I began working with British Youth for Christ as a school's evangelist at age twenty-three, YFC's president was Clive Calver, an ardent Tozer fan. He encouraged all us staff members to saturate our minds and hearts in Tozer's writings—thirty books in all. The first Tozer book I read was *The Knowledge of the Holy,* and although it's short, it's extremely powerful and challenging.

Tozer writes, "What comes to our mind when we think about God is the most important thing about us." Think about that for a moment. Don't rush past. That's a huge statement. *What comes to our mind when we think about God is the most important thing about us.* If we see God as our Lord, our Savior, our provider, the lover of our souls, then that will affect how we live, how we love, and what consumes us.

When I started to date Barry, all I knew about him was that he was a Christian, he was cute—very cute—he dressed well, and his car was blue. As our relationship progressed, I learned so much more about him. I learned that he is very creative and loves to work in the production side of television, special events, and video shoots. He also loves fried chicken, salsa and chips, and Scooby Doo. I learned he is honest, funny, and a great father. I continue to learn things about him, and as I see him inviting God to impact every area of his life, I love him more.

If you feel that your heart has grown a little cold toward God or that you don't have any passion or fire left, then let me reintroduce you to the one whom your heart, soul, mind, and whole being longs for.

> And this is my prayer: that your love may abound more
> and more in knowledge and depth of insight, so that you

may be able to discern what is best and may be pure and blameless until the day of Christ. (Philippians 1:9-10)

EL ELYON—THE GOD WHO IS IN CONTROL OF ALL THINGS

One of my dearest friends in life is Marilyn Meberg. She has been a college professor and a therapist and is currently an author and part of the Women of Faith speaker team. Several years ago Marilyn's husband, Ken, was diagnosed with pancreatic cancer, one of the most difficult cancers to treat. In her 2002 message for Women of Faith, she addressed how painful it was to watch Ken's battle with this ravenous beast that decimated his body and finally took his life. One of the adjectives she used to describe this experience was *sensational*—not a term usually used by those who find themselves in such a black hole. Marilyn explained that although it was far from sensational to watch her darling husband suffer, what was sensational was the presence of our sovereign God and the deep peace that she and Ken experienced, knowing that God is in control and very present at all moments of life—including the most difficult. That is what is expressed in the name El Elyon—God the Most High, ruler of the universe, the God who is in control of all things.

We find this name for God in the Old Testament over and over again. The book of Daniel presents a powerful example through the lives of three Hebrew men who were held in captivity in Babylon at the same time as Daniel was a captive. Their names were Shadrach, Meshach, and Abednego. These courageous Jews refused to worship anyone but the one true God. Their faith infuriated King Nebuchadnezzar.

"Is it true, Shadrach, Meshach and Abednego, that you do not serve my gods or worship the image of gold I have set up?" (Daniel 3:14). They acknowledged that was true.

King Nebuchadnezzar had commissioned an image of gold, ninety feet high and nine feet wide, and set it up on the plain of Dura in the province of Babylon. The king told the three men that if they continued to refuse to worship his gods and his gold creation, he would have them thrown into a furnace. What god would be able to help them then? he asked.

They replied, "O Nebuchadnezzar, we do not need to defend ourselves before you in this matter. If we are thrown into the blazing furnace, the God we serve is able to save us from it, and he will rescue us from your hand, O king. But even if he does not, we want you to know, O king, that we will not serve your gods or worship the image of gold you have set up" (3:16-18).

Their tremendous faith in the sovereignty of God was clearly expressed in their response. They had no doubt that God could pluck them out of the flames, but whether he did or not wouldn't change their allegiance to him, because he is El Elyon, the God who in his sovereignty is in control at all times.

The king ordered the furnace keeper to intensify the heat to seven times its normal temperature. The three friends were tied up by the strongest men in the palace guard and tossed into the blistering inferno. The heat from the furnace was so intense that the guards who threw them in were killed instantly by the scalding waves of fiery air that were released when the furnace door was opened. Nebuchadnezzar, standing by to see this small resistance movement incinerated, was instead a guest at a miracle. What this unholy king saw terrified him, because suddenly there were *four* men in the furnace, walking around, unbound, and talking together. He described one as looking like a god.

"Nebuchadnezzar then approached the opening of the blazing furnace and shouted, 'Shadrach, Meshach and Abednego, servants of the Most High God, come out! Come here!' So Shadrach, Meshach and Abednego came out of the fire" (3:26). This extraordinary utterance is clear evidence that even an enraged pagan king could see that the God of these mere mortals was the Most High God, El Elyon.

The king's initial question to the three men is a great question for us today: "What god will be able to rescue you from my hand?" If we end up in the fire, who will be able to rescue us? If our prayers don't seem to be answered, if our children walk away from God, if our health is decimated, who will help us? The answer is clear: El Elyon.

The trio in the furnace give us a beautiful and profound picture of what trusting in God's "rescue" looks like. They acknowledged that God could either snatch them *out* of the flames or be with them *in* the flames. They willingly accepted however God chose to help them.

If I ask my son to help me bake a cake, he might suggest adding all sorts of things that don't belong in a traditional cake recipe but could be fun. If, however, he wanted to add gravel and wood shavings, I would resist his help at that point, knowing that I have better information at my fingertips as an adult than he does as a child. So often we associate the word *help* with people coming alongside us and doing what we ask them to do, but when we turn to our sovereign God for help, we are asked to bow our knee to whatever that rescue looks like, because he is El Elyon, and he knows what he is about. I take great comfort in the sovereignty of God because of his character, his goodness, his mercy, and his grace. God has no favorites. He loves all his children with equal passion, even if at times it seems to us that we have been overlooked.

We live in a litigious and consumer-satisfaction culture. If something or someone fails us, we sue. If a product does not live up to its commercial hype, we return it. I believe that this virus has infected our relationship with God. If he does not perform as we expect, we take him to an internal court. If our prayers are not answered the way we want, we turn away from God or at least retrieve some of the control we have given to him and determine to take up the slack ourselves. One of the greatest hurdles that we face as believers in the twenty-first century is to reject the self-serving culture we live in and surrender everything to almighty God. God is either sovereign, or he is not El

Elyon. He may not answer as we want him to, but he is still in control, and he is good.

Does it seem as if I am glossing over the pain of your life with quick and easy platitudes? Perhaps some seemingly senseless tragedy has altered the landscape of your life forever. I am not advocating a life of pretense where we stuff our suffering under a rug with a parroting of, "God is in control," as if that is what God wants to squeeze out of us. What I long for in the hearts and minds of those who love God is that we would embrace two things that are true even when they seem to contradict one another: Life is hard, and God is good.

In the fall of 2002 we had a conference in Detroit, Michigan. I talked about Christian's early impressions of kindergarten and how much fun he was having. At the end of the evening a woman showed me a picture of her son. He was Christian's age. I remembered that I had met her the previous year and that she had asked me to pray for him as he was very sick.

"He would have started kindergarten too this fall," she said, "but he died of leukemia in the spring."

"I am so sorry," I said. "I revel in the fun things Christian enjoys, never thinking that someone is sitting and listening through the filter of grief and loss."

"Don't be sorry. You should talk about him. I love to hear your stories. Yes, I cried tonight, and at times I feel a fresh tear in a barely healing wound. But what you said is true. Life is hard, but I still believe that God is good. I still believe that God is good."

One of the most powerful statements of confidence in this aspect of the character of God comes from the mouth of Christ at a crucial moment during his arrest and trial. In his gospel, Mark gives an account of Christ's condemnation before the high priest, Caiaphas. The high priest had no authority to carry out a death sentence under Roman law, and it was very important to the Jewish religious leaders that Jesus die under Roman law. Jewish execution was by stoning, but if you were condemned under Roman law, you were crucified. That would put Jesus, whom they considered to be a blasphemer, under the curse of God and surely end his insidious influence. (See Deuteronomy 21:22-23.)

I find it wonderful that the very thing Christ's enemies pressed for in a demonic effort to finally discredit him had quite the opposite effect. *His curse became our blessing.* "Christ redeemed us from the curse of the law by becoming a curse for us, for it is written: 'Cursed is everyone who is hung on a tree'" (Galatians 3:13).

To get the sentence that the high priest wanted, it was necessary to transfer the case to Pontius Pilate, the Roman governor of Judea. According to his custom, Pilate was in Jerusalem to keep order during the Passover feast. From the beginning of the hearing, Pilate was torn between upsetting the Jews, which was the last thing he wanted during a holy week, and condemning an innocent person. Pilate had little doubt of Christ's innocence or of the evil intent of his accusers. When he finally questioned Jesus, it was without the Jewish entourage that had dragged him there. The Jewish delegation wouldn't enter the courtroom, because entering a Gentile home or business meant that they were under the curse of seven days' defilement. As the Passover was pending, they would have no wish to be excluded from the feast because they were ceremonially unclean.

Pilate asked Jesus who he was and where he had come from. When Jesus refused to speak, Pilate said to him, "Don't you realize I have power either to free you or to crucify you?" (John 19:10). Pilate wanted Jesus to work with him, to help him out of this impossible situation. Jesus would not. When Pilate threatened Jesus by wielding his power over him, Jesus answered, "You would have no power over me if it were not given to you from above. Therefore the one who handed me over to you is guilty of a greater sin" (John 19:11).

What a definitive statement on the sovereignty of God! This is Jesus worshiping at the feet of El Elyon. He was saying, "You may think you hold my life in your hands, but my life is in the hands of God alone. Any authority you have was given by him, and he could remove it in an instant."

Are you in a situation where someone is out to do you harm, to discredit your name or stain your reputation? Take heart! God is in control, and he will be your vindicator if you will rest in him. That's so hard to do. If you are like me, you want to do something about it yourself, but a belief in the sovereignty of God calls for our relinquishing control.

We live in an unfair world where people can inflict treacherous wounds. When I worked at the Christian Broadcasting Network, someone lied about me in a way that pierced me like a sword in my side. My initial reaction was to try to undo what had been done and then ask God to deal with the person in question. I did not mean deal lovingly and kindly; I wanted God to "get him good." When he didn't seem to do that, I was outraged. "God, you love me, and you know it was a lie. Do something!" He did. God began to work on *my* heart, which was not what I had in mind at all.

It became clear to me that while we can right some situations, there are others we have to let go of, believing that God is in control, he knows what is true, and he loves us. It is easy to parrot the well-loved scripture "And we know that in all things God works for the good of those who love him, who have been called according to his purpose" (Romans 8:28). But what does that mean? If we review the verse in the context of the whole chapter, we get a clearer picture. The chapter ends with the glorious assertion that nothing can separate us from God's love. "For I am convinced that neither death nor life, neither angels nor demons, neither the present nor the future, nor any powers, neither height nor depth, nor anything else in all creation, will be able to separate us from the love of God that is in Christ Jesus our Lord" (8:38-39). The apostle Paul doesn't sidestep the fact that bad things happen to God's people. A few verses earlier we read, "Who shall separate us from the love of Christ? Shall trouble or hardship or persecution or famine or nakedness or danger or sword?" (8:35).

Even for God's beloved children, life on this earth can be heart-breaking, but those who put their trust in the Lord never lose the last round. Therefore, we can rest in his sovereignty, refusing an end run around our inevitable suffering. A belief in the sovereignty of God means that whether we understand what is happening or not, whether God seems silent or not, whether evil seems to be winning over good or not, we gather up our faith and say to God, "I love you. I trust you. This hurts me, but I know that you know the end from the beginning and have my good at heart, so I say Yes! to you and No! to trying to grab control and fix everything myself."

Christian had strep throat in the winter of 2001, so Barry and I took him to see his pediatrician. Dr. Ladd told us that he could have a course of pills and that he would feel better in about a week, or he could have a shot and start to feel better the next day. Christian asked me, "Mom, if I have the shot, will it hurt?"

"Yes, it will, darling, but you will start to feel so much better soon."

"What do you think I should do, Mom?" he asked, his eyes filling with tears.

"If I were you, I would have the shot, but whatever you choose is fine," I replied.

"Then I'll have the shot," he announced.

It did hurt. I held his hand, and he squeezed mine tightly as tears ran down his face. I know that Christian didn't understand why it had to hurt so bad, but he trusted that, even when it made no sense to him, I would never put him through something that wasn't for his ultimate good.

We often want an easy way out, but that's not always available or wise. The men in the furnace trusted their sovereign God and refused an easy way out. Jesus trusted his Father and refused an easy way out. All of them knew that this could cost their lives, but either God is sovereign over all, or he is not sovereign at all. Scripture doesn't tell us that everything will go as we would like but rather that God is always in control, regardless. Not our enemies, known or unknown, not chance or fate, not you, not me, but God, El Elyon, is in control, and he is good. He will always have the last say, and nothing, absolutely nothing, can separate us from his love.

For forty years the children of Israel wandered in the desert. Forty years is a long time. Add forty years to the age you are at the moment to put it in perspective. Their story, told in the book of Exodus, is a litany of complaints, sarcasm, anger, idol worship, disobedience, immorality, and debauchery. It is also a history of the relentless love of God and his patience with his people. When I am afraid, I can so easily revert to sarcasm or anger as a camouflage for how vulnerable I feel. In answer to the desert wanderers' sarcasm, Moses went straight to the real problem: fear. "Moses answered the people, 'Do not be afraid. Stand firm and you will see the deliverance the LORD will bring you today. The Egyptians you see today you will never see again. The LORD will fight for you; you need only to be still' " (Exodus 14:13-14).

"You need only to be still." Other translations say, "While you keep silent" (NASB).

If life seems out of control to you, rest quietly in the truth that God is sovereign. Examine your own life within the context of this knowledge of who God is. Do you believe that God is in control, at this moment, of all things to do with you? You are not a victim left to the tides of people or circumstances. It may seem that way, but take hope and receive the peace of El Elyon.

JEHOVAH-TSIDKENU—THE LORD WHO IS OUR RIGHTEOUSNESS IN ALL THINGS

It was past ten o'clock, and I was tired. At Women of Faith conferences I speak on Friday night and then go up to my book table to meet anyone who wants to talk or have a book signed. I usually try to get out of the arena by ten, as we have an early start on Saturday. That gives me about an hour to be available to listen, to talk, to laugh, or to cry. On this particular Friday images of a hot bath and a pizza danced before my eyes as the line of women in front of me dwindled...until I saw her. A woman was standing against the wall near my table. Her head was lowered, and I could see that she was shredding a tissue in her hands. I know that in a crowd of fifteen thousand women I can't possibly get to everyone who might want to talk, but I felt a strong prompting from God to talk to this woman. I stood beside her for a few moments, then she grabbed my hand. She grabbed it the way a drowning woman would cling to a rope. It took her some time to be able to talk.

"I shouldn't be here," she said. "I have no right to be here."

"What do you mean?" I asked. "You have as much a right as anyone else."

"No I don't." She wouldn't look up.

"You don't have to tell me anything," I said, "but if you want a listening ear, I'm here."

The story poured out like poison excised from a wound. She was having an affair.

"I'm married. I have two beautiful children. I am in hell. What should I do?" She told me that her husband knew and was willing to forgive her, but she believed that she had destroyed all that was good in their lives and still felt drawn to the other man. We talked for a long time. She asked me what I would do if I were in her place.

"That's impossible for me to answer," I said. "I'm not you. I'm not carrying your pain and guilt, desire and longings. I'm not living your story. But I can tell you what I think the right path would be." She raised her head and looked at me.

"Do you love your husband?" I asked. She nodded. "Tell this other man that it's over. There is no future for you together; there is only pain and heartache. Take your husband at his word, get into some good counseling, and start to rebuild your life. It won't be easy, but you're not alone in this. Christ is with you. He will help you face all that is true about yourself."

"I know what's true!" she said bitterly. "I'm an adulteress. I have ruined everything. Nothing will ever be the same again."

I held her as she wept and then recited these words to her, " 'Come now, let us reason together,' says the LORD. 'Though your sins are like scarlet, they shall be as white as snow; though they are red as crimson, they shall be like wool' " (Isaiah 1:18).

I gave her my e-mail address and wrote a few more verses in a book that I prayed would help her in the tough days ahead.

One year later we were holding a conference in the same city. On Friday night when Barry and I got back to the hotel, he gave me a note. "Someone asked me to give this to you. She didn't have time to wait."

The note was from the same woman. I wept with joy as I read what God has done in her life, her marriage, and her family.

I saw her the next day. "You know you look like a different woman," I said.

"I feel like a different woman. Only God could have done that. I feel clean."

I began this book looking at the confusion we face when we imagine that God loves us based on our performance. That's never truer than when we have sinned and our shame drags us away from God's presence because we are unclean. The truth from God's Word is clear, however: Even on our best days, we have no righteousness of our own. There was no righteousness in Mother Teresa apart from God. There is no righteousness in Dr. Billy Graham apart from God. "There is no one righteous, not even one," quotes the apostle Paul from Psalm 14 (Romans 3:10).

That is the clarion call of the cross. We cannot save ourselves; we cannot keep the law in our own strength. We will never be good enough to see God's face. So God sent Jesus Christ, the sinless Lamb, to bear the stain of all our sin, all our evil and selfish choices. When we enter into relationship with Christ, we accept this gift of grace, for that's what it is—a gift. We didn't work to earn it, and we don't have to work to keep it. It is God's gift to us in Christ. "For in the gospel a righteousness from God is revealed," Paul says, "a righteousness that is by faith from first to last, just as it is written: 'The righteous will live by faith'" (Romans 1:17).

That has always been God's plan: to make a way for those who deserve no way. We see it in the Old Testament in the life of Noah. The Genesis account begins with the description of Noah's being "righteous." "Noah was a righteous man, blameless among the people of his time, and he walked with God" (Genesis 6:9). The story not only demonstrates why God sent a flood but also triumphantly acknowledges why God saved Noah. The message is clear. God saved Noah because he walked with God. The picture of Noah that emerges becomes a model of the kind of life that finds grace in the sight of the Lord: simple obedience to God's commands and trust in his provision by faith.

Where does this strike you in your life today? Perhaps like that desperate woman who shared her secret with me, you feel that you have sinned too much. Abortion, adultery, drug or alcohol abuse, sexual immorality, deceit—each has its own peculiar stigma, and the shame attached brings down the weight of the world on a human soul. Jesus died for those sins, all those sins, every one of those sins.

Perhaps you feel pretty good about yourself in the righteousness stakes. I used to. I had a complacent smugness about the things I had never done. I was a very judgmental teenager. After the month I spent in the psychiatric unit years later, I viewed life completely differently. I saw that my suppressed anger, my sarcasm, my pride were revolting in God's eyes. But even as I wept over my spiritual blindness, I was invited to wade into the river of Christ's righteousness and be washed clean, standing shoulder to shoulder with other forgiven sinners. The prophet's words became a balm: "I delight greatly in the LORD; my soul rejoices in my God. For he has clothed me with garments of salvation and arrayed me in a robe of righteousness, as a bridegroom adorns his head like a priest, and as a bride adorns herself with her jewels" (Isaiah 61:10).

We have only begun to scratch the surface of all that our great God has revealed about himself. We cannot love a God we do not know, but God longs to be known by us. That has always been his heart: relationship. Out of relationship with him springs the desire to love him with heart, soul, mind, and strength. It is only in relationship with him that we can love ourselves and love others as we have been called to love them.

ADONAI—THE GOD WHO IS LORD OF ALL THINGS

In Old Testament times, names were weighty, packed with significance. Your name expressed or defined who you essentially were, and so your name revealed a lot about you before you ever said a word. So too with this awesome title for God, Adonai. The Hebrew text uses the word *Adonay,* meaning the Lord, Sovereign, the one true God, Lord of lords, the highest power or authority in heaven, on earth, and under the earth.

This name appears the first time in the Old Testament on Abram's lips in Genesis 15:2: "But Abram said, 'O Sovereign [Adonai] LORD, what can you give me since I remain childless and the one who will inherit my estate is Eliezer of Damascus?'"

This was the first time that Abram actually spoke to God. He had heard from God before, but here he responded to God. In his response he acknowledged him as Adonai, Lord and Master. Even within that statement of faith, Abram's questions began the dialogue that continues with us. That issue, central to our faith and hope in God, is his apparent delay in fulfilling his promises. Abram's predicament was like that of later generations of God's people, as he, too, had to wait in faith for the fulfillment of the promise. All the blessings and security of relationship with God come from bending our knees to this truth that God is Lord and Master—and he is Lord and Master in his time, not in ours.

To acknowledge God as Lord demands a certain response. To use that name requires our honoring that name. To use that name and then disobey would anger God, as Moses discovered. In his encounter with God recorded in Exodus 3, God confronted him in a bush aflame in the desert, but the bush was not being consumed by the fire. God spoke to him out of the inferno, telling him that he had heard the cry of his people held captive in Egypt and would send Moses to deliver them. Moses was terrified at the thought of returning to Egypt, a country he fled after murdering a man and burying his body in the sand.

God was persistent. Moses was stubborn. "O Lord, please send someone else to do it," Moses whined. "Then the LORD's anger burned against Moses" (Exodus 4:13-14).

Why was God so angry? Surely he could understand the dread of a man returning to a place soaked in bad memories. God was angry because Moses addressed him as Lord, Adonai, and then refused to live under that lordship. It would be like a man signing up to be a marine. He undergoes extensive, expensive training, month after month, year after year. Finally it's time for him to serve his country, but even as he receives his orders, he tells his commanding officer, "I don't think I want to do this, sir. Thanks for the opportunity, but I don't feel really up to it today, sir. What about Smith over there, sir? He's great at this stuff, sir."

That is a weak example, but my point is simply this: If we call God *Lord,* then we have to live within all the truth that name implies, or else we should not call him Lord at all. Jesus revisited this issue, according to Luke's gospel.

Why do you call me, "Lord, Lord," and do not do what
I say? I will show you what he is like who comes to me

and hears my words and puts them into practice. He is
like a man building a house, who dug down deep and
laid the foundation on rock. When a flood came, the
torrent struck that house but could not shake it, because
it was well built. But the one who hears my words and
does not put them into practice is like a man who built
a house on the ground without a foundation. The
moment the torrent struck that house, it collapsed and
its destruction was complete. (Luke 6:46-49)

I think it's hard for us to grasp the significance and weight of calling God *Lord.* We have no frame of reference for this kind of authority. My sister is a teacher in an elementary school in Scotland, and the
tales she tells of the total disregard for authority that seems to exist in
many of our young people today horrify me. When I was at that level
of education, my classmates and I would never have dreamed of being
disrespectful to a teacher, but now part of the unraveling of our culture
is the acceptance of rebellion in our children. If they have no respect
for human authority, how can we expect them to bend their knees to
God? I think I'm pretty easy on Christian. I don't wrestle with him on
small issues; I choose carefully which hills are worth dying on. But the
one thing I will not tolerate is disrespect to his father and me, to others,
or to God.

The deterioration of our culture is seen too in our casual friendship
with God. If we water down *Lord* to mean nothing more than *Buddy,*
we are in serious trouble. When we minimize the ultimate authority of
our sovereign Lord, we border on idolatry where our opinion holds
equal weight with God's.

The pursuit to know God and to acknowledge him as Lord of all
things has always been controversial. It has cost some Christians their
lives even at the hands of those who claim the same allegiance to God.
In the seventeenth century, Miguel de Molinos, a Spanish theologian,

was thrown into prison for asserting that our ultimate call as believers is an allegiance to God alone and a total surrender of our wills to his. This was seen as a threat to the church and her authority, and the Inquisition had de Molinos thrown into prison, where he eventually died. But he was right. I know he died knowing that he was right. God is God all by himself. We have lost some of the wonder of that. I love the fact that God encourages us to call him Abba, Father, but the warmth of that tender relationship should not diminish our reverence of his lordship.

It's interesting to contrast the response of Moses and the response of the prophet Isaiah as the Lord confronted them both. Moses said, "Lord…I can't do this!" Isaiah's reaction to the revelation of God was radically different.

> "Woe to me!" I cried. "I am ruined! For I am a man of unclean lips, and I live among a people of unclean lips, and my eyes have seen the King, the LORD Almighty."
>
> Then one of the seraphs flew to me with a live coal in his hand, which he had taken with tongs from the altar. With it he touched my mouth and said, "See, this has touched your lips; your guilt is taken away and your sin atoned for."
>
> Then I heard the voice of the Lord saying, "Whom shall I send? And who will go for us?"
>
> And I said, "Here am I. Send me!" (Isaiah 6:5-8)

I identify with Moses: "I can't do it."

I long to be like Isaiah: "Here am I, send me."

In the modern classic *The Christian's Secret of a Happy Life*, Hannah Whitall Smith writes, "I remember reading once somewhere this sentence, 'Perfect obedience would be perfect happiness, if only we had perfect confidence in the power we were obeying.' I remember being struck with the saying, as the revelation of a possible, although hitherto undreamed-of way of happiness; and often afterwards, through all the lawlessness and willfulness of my life, did that saying recur to me as the vision of a rest, and yet of a possible development, that would soothe and at the same time satisfy all my yearnings."

This is a "way of happiness"—to finally acknowledge that God is Lord and we are his people, so all is well. We can have perfect confidence in the God we are obeying. Jesus came to show us what God is like and to put human flesh on eternal spirit. His submission to the ultimate authority of God, even to the point of barbaric execution, is staggering.

Stop for a moment and reflect on the peace that comes with relinquishing control of all the areas of your life to God.

Are you concerned about your husband or wife or your lack of a husband or a wife?

Are you worried about your children or the fact that your maternal arms are still empty?

As you look to the future, are you afraid?

Sometimes life feels out of control. We are almost afraid to pick up the newspaper or turn on the television. Nation fights against nation; famine, disease, and floods ravage the earth; threats are being broadcast from every corner of the planet. But we love and serve a God who is in control of everything. Jesus said, "When you hear of wars and revolutions, do not be frightened. These things must happen first, but the end will not come right away" (Luke 21:9).

Whatever the media says, God is in control.

Whatever your circumstances say, God is in control.

Whatever your own mind says, God is in control, and he loves you.

Let's bring all of who we are and all whom we love and place them intentionally under the lordship of Christ.

> I lift up my eyes to the hills—
> where does my help come from?

My help comes from the LORD,
    the Maker of heaven and earth.

He will not let your foot slip—
    he who watches over you will not slumber;
indeed, he who watches over Israel
    will neither slumber nor sleep.

The LORD watches over you—
    the LORD is your shade at your right hand;
the sun will not harm you by day,
    nor the moon by night.

The LORD will keep you from all harm—
    he will watch over your life;
the LORD will watch over your coming and going
    both now and forevermore. (Psalm 121)

The LORD watches over all who love him.

PSALM 145:20

Guide me, O thou great Jehovah
Pilgrim through this barren land;
I am weak, but Thou art mighty;
Hold me with Thy powerful hand;
Bread of heaven, bread of heaven;
Feed me till I want no more;
Feed me till I want no more.

PETER WILLIAMS

Because of the LORD'S great love we are not consumed,
for his compassions never fail.
They are new every morning;
great is your faithfulness.
I say to myself, "The LORD is my portion;
therefore I will wait for him."

LAMENTATIONS 3:22-24

CHAPTER FOUR

SOMEONE TO WATCH OVER ME

Trusting in His Faithfulness

We have looked at our majestic and sovereign God who is in control of all things, but he is also our loving protector who sees us, guides us, and longs to give us his peace in all the moments of our lives.

Peace is the prerogative of those who trust in God. The peace that he gives us holds us through the sunshine and storms of life because it's not dependent on things going our way. It is wholly dependent on whose way we are on.

Various theologians have identified at least forty-five names for God, but in this chapter I want to focus on three that highlight his faithfulness and ever-present love:

Jehovah Shalom: the God who brings peace to all things

El Roi: the God who sees all things

Jehovah-raah: the God who shepherds us through all things

JEHOVAH SHALOM—THE GOD WHO BRINGS PEACE TO ALL THINGS

I had been a patient in the psychiatric ward of a hospital close to Washington, D.C., for two weeks. I found the initial days terrifying, but by the second week I had begun to settle into the routine of life in this unit. Every morning the patients gathered in the lounge, held hands, and prayed for God's blessing, protection, and guidance for that day. Then we moved on to group therapy or individual counseling. As with many of my fears, the reality of the experience of being a patient and facing the hard issues of life that presented themselves as a roadblock on my journey was far less overwhelming than my imagination portrayed. By the second week I was grateful for the help and guidance I was receiving. I had made some friends among the other patients and had even been voted entertainment secretary!

The first sign to me that I was feeling a little better was when I became aware that I was singing one evening. I realized then that I had not sung in some time. To some that might seem an insignificant sign, but it was a lighthouse beacon to me. All my life I have sung as I go through my day. I sing in the shower, in the car, while I'm fixing dinner. Now here I was walking down the corridor of a psychiatric hospital and singing quietly. I was headed to the nurses' station to ask if I could get my hair dryer out for half an hour. (All patients in psych wards surrender anything that could be potentially dangerous to themselves or to another patient, but usually you are allowed to check them out under supervision.)

As I got closer to the desk, I saw two women who looked about my age, and they were supporting an older woman who was silently weeping while the nurse began the admission process. My heart went out to her. I recognized that look of terror at being admitted to a psychiatric unit. I stopped in my tracks and decided to come back later. This family seemed to need time alone. As I turned to leave, I heard one of the women call my name. I turned back to see the woman plead with her mother to look up.

"Mom, look! God gave us our miracle!"

I had no idea what was happening, but instinctively I moved toward the mom. She looked up at me, cried out, and threw her arms around my neck. She was crying, the daughters were crying, and I was crying, but I was the only one who had no idea why we were crying!

After a little while we all sat down, and the daughters explained. They told me that their father had abused their mother most of their married life. "He broke her jaw once," the elder daughter said. "We begged her to leave, but she always said that she took her marriage vows before God seriously and couldn't leave. But finally we persuaded her to leave and get some help before he killed her."

"She was terrified of coming here," the other daughter added. "We prayed for a miracle. We asked God to give Mom a sign as she walked in the door that she was in a safe place."

"How do I fit in?" I asked, genuinely perplexed.

They all laughed. "Don't you know us, Sheila? We're your sisters!"

For a moment I thought, *Wow! I'm worse than I thought I was if I've got two sisters I can't remember.*

Seeing the look of puzzlement in my eyes, they filled in the blanks. "Mom watches *The 700 Club* every day, never misses. It's her source of encouragement," one said. "She prays with you every day, Sheila. It's kind of a family joke that Mom has three daughters: my sister and me, and then there is you! Don't you see? There's nothing that God could have done to make Mom feel more at home than to have her met at the door by her 'third' daughter."

I love that God did that. I could have been a patient there any month; this broken, frightened woman could have finally agreed to get help at another time. But God put us together at that precise moment so we could walk together through a dark valley and find his peace.

In the Old and New Testaments, God's peace is seen as a gift not to those who are fearless but to those who tremble with fear, wondering if they will survive. When the disciples huddled together like wounded birds in an upper room after the crucifixion, they were sick at heart. Jesus, their one and only hope on this earth, had been butchered before their eyes, and they were terrified and hopeless. Cutting through that cloak of despair, Jesus stood before them and said, "Peace be with you" (Luke 24:36). Nothing outside the room had changed, but because Jesus was there, everything had changed. It is the presence of God, not the absence of trouble, that brings peace.

When we are transformed by an encounter with Jehovah Shalom, it's clear to the watching world that the peace we exhibit is from God. He often chooses to show the power of his gift of peace in the most unlikely people. We see that in the life of a timid young man, Gideon, to whom we are introduced in the book of Judges. By the time we meet him in chapter 6, his people, the Israelites, had already fallen into sin four times. They had turned from Jehovah God over and over again in a vain attempt to find for themselves a sense of immediate security by worshiping false gods. They had given themselves over to immorality and spiritual darkness.

One would imagine that after their remarkable deliverance from Egypt, their devotion to God would have been passionate and unswerving, but how quickly they and we forget all that God has done for us. Now they were in trouble yet again. This time they were being threatened by the Midianites, who were about to descend on them like a swarm of locusts. Again they cried out to God to save them. It was a familiar pattern. When they were in trouble, they called out to God to save them. He delivered them in unprecedented, miraculous ways, but before the last hallelujah had fallen into the sand, they turned away from God again and returned to the pigsty of their former choices.

I see myself reflected in those desert wanderers. As long as I am in intimate fellowship with God, I experience a deep peace regardless of the circumstances of my life, but when my life gets so noisy that God's voice is drowned in a sea of "stuff," I feel lost and anxious. There is no wholeness or righteousness in any of us apart from God.

Once more God inclined his ear of mercy to his people as they cried for help. God chose Gideon to be the deliverer of his people. If you study the story, you will see that Gideon was an extremely unlikely choice. He was a small, mousy guy from the smallest tribe, and yet the angel of the Lord addressed him as "mighty warrior." (I imagine that

Gideon must have looked behind him to see whom the angel was talking to!)

When the angel appeared to Gideon, he found him hiding in a wine press, a pit carved out of rocky ground. It was his job to thresh wheat. Normally the threshing floor would be in an exposed area, where the wind would blow the chaff away, but Gideon was working undercover, doing a less than satisfactory job because he was afraid. I'm sure that's why God chose him. Gideon was terrified at the sight of the angel of the Lord, so he asked for proof that the angel was indeed addressing him. (Who else did he think it would be?) He asked the angel if he would hold on for a moment, as he wanted to run back home and prepare a sacrifice. (Can you imagine asking the angel of the Lord to take a seat for a moment!)

The angel agreed and waited. Gideon brought back a young goat and some unleavened bread and placed them on a rock. The angel touched the rock with his staff, and fire appeared from the rock and consumed the sacrifice. Now two things were clear to Gideon: This was indeed the angel of the Lord, and he was in big trouble for doubting in the first place! "When Gideon realized that it was the angel of the LORD, he exclaimed, 'Ah, Sovereign LORD! I have seen the angel of the LORD face to face!' But the LORD said to him, 'Peace! Do not be afraid. You are not going to die.' So Gideon built an altar to the LORD there and called it The LORD is Peace. To this day it stands in Ophrah of the Abiezrites" (Judges 6:22-24).

God told Gideon that he would be the one to deliver God's people but first he must cleanse his own family of their allegiance to the false god Baal. Gideon obeyed and built an altar to Jehovah God set high on a rock. He offered a bull as a sacrifice, an animal usually reserved for Baal. Gideon must have known that he was putting his life in danger, so he made the sacrifice at night when everyone was asleep. The next morning when the people heard what he had done, they demanded Gideon's life. They asked Joash, Gideon's father, to kill his son. Joash responded that if Baal were truly God, he would be able to defend himself. The people waited to see what this mighty god would do to little Gideon. When nothing happened, he suddenly had the ears of his people.

Gideon told them that Jehovah was going to deliver them. He assembled an army of 32,000 men. The Midianites had over 120,000 men. Outnumbered four to one, Gideon was justifiably afraid. He had no idea, however, that God was about to drastically reduce his fighting force. The story's intent is clear. Peace comes not from having a great army but from being obedient to a great God. God told Gideon that he had too many soldiers! If they had defeated the Midianites with 32,000 men, they might have taken the credit for it, so God told Gideon to release any soldiers who were afraid.

Imagine the sight. "All right, men! We are mighty warriors! We will deliver our people! God is with us! We are fearless! Now before we get started, in the unlikely event that any man is afraid, you may leave now."

Twenty-two thousand of the mighty soldiers ran home.

"Whoa! Hold it! Come back! Where are you all going?" With 22,000 soldiers gone, Gideon was now left with 10,000. God told him that he still had too many men. He told Gideon to perform a water test. He was to take all the soldiers to the edge of the river and watch how they drank. He could keep the men who scooped water with their hands and release the men who got down on their knees to drink. Ninety-seven hundred of them knelt down to drink. Three hundred scooped water with their hands. Now he had 300 men against a well-equipped army of 120,000, and in a miraculous way they defeated the Midianites and sent them running in panic, turning on each other in their confusion.

The rest of Gideon's story recorded in the book of Judges is a wonderful reminder of how a faithful God provides for us and grants us peace in the midst of overwhelming circumstances. Apart from the

Lord, Gideon was still the same scared little man with many amazing adventures ahead, but what Gideon learned was to trust Jehovah Shalom, the God of peace.

Circumstances have nothing to do with peace; God's presence does. You can see that joyful truth reflected on the walls of the catacombs in Rome where the following statement is engraved in several places, *"In Christo, in pace."* In Christ, in peace. Whatever you are facing at this moment, God longs to give you his peace.

We live in a time when more and more of us are turning to medication to handle stress and anxiety, and while I am by no means questioning the benefit of psychiatric medications (I am a grateful recipient), I do see a trend to anesthetize our fears rather than bring them all to Christ and hear him speak, "Peace be with you."

> Do not be anxious about anything, but in everything, by prayer and petition, with thanksgiving, present your requests to God. And the peace of God, which transcends all understanding, will guard your hearts and your minds in Christ Jesus. (Philippians 4:6-7)

EL ROI—THE GOD WHO SEES ALL THINGS

"How can God allow this?" she asked me with tears pouring down her cheeks. Her face looked as if she had been crying incessantly. "Doesn't God see what's going on?"

I was speaking at a conference in Chicago. At the end of the evening a woman in her fifties approached me and asked if we could talk. I had heard her story before, poured out through other lips but with the same haunted look of disbelief behind tired eyes. She told me that she had been married for more than twenty years and had raised two fine boys, and now her husband, with a simple "I don't love you anymore," was gone.

"He was a pastor," she continued. "I've lost my home. I can't show my face in church anymore. Where is God? Has he forgotten me?"

This is a familiar refrain. "How long, O LORD, must I call for help, but you do not listen? Or cry out to you, 'Violence!' but you do not save? Why do you make me look at injustice? Why do you tolerate wrong? Destruction and violence are before me; there is strife, and conflict abounds. Therefore the law is paralyzed, and justice never prevails. The wicked hem in the righteous, so that justice is perverted" (Habakkuk 1:2-4).

Have you ever felt abandoned, as if no one knew where you were or what was happening in your life?

Where are you, God?

Do you see me?

Why don't you do something?

In those desperate moments I want to remind you of a woman who felt exactly like that until El Roi, the God who sees everything, showed up and changed her life.

The first time we encounter this name of God is in the book of Genesis. Hagar, servant to Sarai, Abram's wife, uses it. (God had not yet changed their names to Abraham and Sarah.) In frustration that she was unable to conceive and have a child, Sarai asked her husband to sleep with her maid in the hope that she could build a family through her. Hagar became pregnant and, with hormones raging, used her condition to torment her mistress. Sarai was devastated and blamed Abram. He wanted nothing to do with this catfight and told her to do what she wanted with Hagar. Sarai made life so miserable for Hagar that she ran away.

Out in the desert, pregnant and alone in the scorching heat, Hagar encountered an angel of the Lord. The angel told her to go home and apologize to Sarai and submit to her authority. He told her that the child she was carrying was a boy who would be the father of so many descendants that she couldn't begin to count them.

Hagar was deeply moved by the words of the angel. She was more profoundly impacted by the fact that God saw her, knew where she was, and knew all about her situation. She was dying out in the hot desert, alone, abandoned by human flesh, but not out of divine view. "She gave this name to the LORD who spoke to her: 'You are the God who sees me,' for she said, 'I have now seen the One who sees me'" (Genesis 16:13).

Scripture is full of references to the truth that God sees everything.

> His eyes are on the ways of men; he sees their every
> step. (Job 34:21)

> From heaven the LORD looks down and sees all
> mankind. (Psalm 33:13)

> But the eyes of the LORD are on those who fear him, on
> those whose hope is in his unfailing love. (Psalm 33:18)

> But when you pray, go into your room, close the door
> and pray to your Father, who is unseen. Then your
> Father, who sees what is done in secret, will reward you.
> (Matthew 6:6)

God took care of Hagar's every need. "Then God opened her eyes and she saw a well of water" (Genesis 21:19). That's my prayer for you and for me. As we sit thirsting for life, may God open the eyes of our hearts to see the well of living water that he has poured into those who love him.

Lana Bateman has traveled with Women of Faith for five years as an intercessor. On Fridays before the doors are open, she spends several hours in the arena praying that each woman who walks through the doors will be aware of the love of God. She prays with every one of the speakers and singers that we will be sensitive to the Holy Spirit's moving in and through our lives. She told me a story recently that reminded me of Hagar and an encounter with a God who sees all.

Lana had been invited by a group of women in England to come teach them about listening to the voice of God in prayer. It was a small group, and financially they were not able to underwrite her trip. Lana had little income at the time but felt that God wanted her to go. Finally she was able to obtain a standby ticket and told the women that if God wanted her to be on the flight that she would be on it.

As she sat in the departure lounge, she could see that it was clearly a busy flight. Lana asked the agent at the desk the probability of getting on the flight. He told her it looked impossible. Coach was fully checked in. Lana began walking back toward the terminal entrance, a lone figure in a crowded airport, knowing that in human terms things seemed bleak. But she rested in her conviction that God, El Roi, saw his daughter and had her itinerary in his hand.

She heard an announcement over the intercom calling her back to the ticket counter. She rushed back through security, knowing that the flight was due to leave in a short time. The ticket agent told her that a space had opened up but she would have to hurry. She arrived at the gate just in time to see the doors close. Lana stood looking through the window at the plane pulling away from the gate. There was nothing she could do.

Then she became aware of a man shouting something and turned to see an employee from El Al, the airline of Israel, waving his ticket in the air and talking intensely to the agents behind the desk. The agent at the gate radioed the plane, and before Lana knew what was happening, she and this man were taken down some steps onto the Tarmac, met by a car, and driven to the plane. Steps were rolled over, and the doors were opened. When a slightly bemused Lana got to the top, she was told that the only seat left was in first class!

Now I'm not suggesting that the next time you fly you buy a standby ticket, trusting that God will reward you with a first-class seat!

But I think Lana's experience is a lovely example of God's seeing his daughter, knowing her heart, and just as he did for Hagar, making a way in the desert.

> Think not thou canst sigh a sigh,
> And thy Maker is not by:
> Think not thou canst weep a tear,
> And thy Maker is not near.
>
> Oh He gives to us His joy,
> That our grief He may destroy:
> Till our grief is fled and gone
> He doth sit by us and moan.
> —William Blake

God sees all.

Are you concerned about a child who has wandered off?

God sees.

Do you find it hard to speak up for yourself, and so your voice is never heard?

God sees.

Do you feel unloved, abandoned, and alone?

God sees.

> Where can I go from your Spirit?
>   Where can I flee from your presence?
> If I go up to the heavens, you are there;
>   if I make my bed in the depths, you are there.
> If I rise on the wings of the dawn,
>   if I settle on the far side of the sea,
> even there your hand will guide me,
>   your right hand will hold me fast.

If I say, "Surely the darkness will hide me
   and the light become night around me,"
even the darkness will not be dark to you;
   the night will shine like the day,
   for darkness is as light to you." (Psalm 139:7-12)

JEHOVAH-RAAH—THE GOD WHO SHEPHERDS US THROUGH ALL THINGS

I had never been to court before, and as a fan of the television show *Law and Order,* I was anticipating that this morning's venture would be dramatic and fun. I had no idea that it would turn into such a sad day.

My husband's last name is Pfaehler; Christian's name is Christian Walsh Pfaehler. Barry has hated his name since he was a child. Through the years he has endured endless teasing and mispronunciations.

Failure.

Faffler.

Poffler.

After the death of his father, Barry talked to me about changing Christian's name and his name to Walsh. I was hesitant to make such a move, but as time went by, I saw that this was very important to him. We decided that if we were going to do this, we needed to do it before Christian started school. We filled in the required paperwork and were given a date to appear before the civil court judge. At nine o'clock that morning we lined up with twenty or thirty others outside courtroom number two. We were told that one of us should go in and listen for our case to be called. I went in while Barry and Christian sat on a bench in the hallway.

I looked around the room and tried to guess why each person was there. All my guesses were sadly wrong. We rose as one when the judge came in. He took his place behind a solemn sturdy desk and began to read the cases on the docket for that morning. He checked to see that all the lawyers were present with their clients, and then he began. "I have two name-change requests for today, but before I get to that, I'll cover the ten noncontested divorces." Within a matter of thirty minutes ten families were legally split in two by a simple signature.

I watched an old woman make her way to the witness stand as she leaned on a cane. Her marriage of thirty-two years was over. A young girl who had been married for only six months, a taxi driver, a man who looked absolutely beaten by life—one by one they stood before the judge and heard the words, "The divorce is granted."

A woman stood with her attorney and begged the judge for a hearing to change child-custody decisions made three years prior. "I'm not a drug addict anymore. I want my children!"

Everyone else in the courtroom seemed numb to the soul splintering that was taking place, but I wept. I heard the judge call my name, and I quickly grabbed Barry and Christian from outside. The three of us stood before the bench.

"Are you requesting a name change because of a divorce?" the judge asked.

"No sir, we just want to have the same name," Barry answered.

The change was granted and entered.

"When he saw the crowds," Matthew wrote of Christ, "he had compassion on them, because they were harassed and helpless, like sheep without a shepherd" (Matthew 9:36). When I read the morning paper or watch the evening news, that's what I see: lost sheep without a shepherd. We have looked at some of the majestic, powerful names of God, but always within this glorious holiness we have a tender shepherd, a sweet companion who will walk with us through this life.

Are you in need of a shepherd today?

Are you tired of trying to be strong?

Do you long for a place to rest?

Jehovah-raah is our God, and he will shepherd us through all things.

I have known the Twenty-third Psalm since I was a child. I love the gentle pastoral images and David's confidence in his eternal relationship with God. It's worth noting, however, where the Twenty-third Psalm is placed. It comes right after what Charles Spurgeon calls "The Psalm of the Cross."

> My God, my God, why have you forsaken me?
> (Psalm 22:1)

Spurgeon wrote in his book *The Treasury of David*, "It is only after we have read, 'My God, my God, why have you forsaken me!' that we come to 'The Lord is my Shepherd.' We must by experience know the value of the blood-shedding and see the sword awakened against the Shepherd, before we shall be able truly to know the sweetness of the good Shepherd's care."

As I reflect back on my morning in court, I see the only hope for such a broken, scattered, and bloodied flock. Because God became flesh and walked among us, we have a Shepherd who knows our pain—not by theory but by brutal, nightmarish experience. I wanted to stand up in that courtroom and say, "You are not alone! There is One who cares for you and would carry you. He swallowed all of hell's foul stench so that you can find green pastures again, so that your soul can be restored."

Psalm 23 is a peculiar treasure, a carefully placed jewel, a gift from God. You might want to read the psalmist's words out loud. That's how God's people in Old Testament times prayed the psalms. They declared them to their own ears, to those who would listen, and to the invisible forces of heaven and hell.

> The LORD is my shepherd; I shall not be in want.
>   He makes me lie down in green pastures,
>   he leads me beside quiet waters,
>   he restores my soul.

He guides me in paths of righteousness
>for his name's sake.
Even though I walk
>through the valley of the shadow of death,
I will fear no evil,
>for you are with me;
your rod and your staff,
>they comfort me.

You prepare a table before me
>in the presence of my enemies.
You anoint my head with oil;
>my cup overflows.
Surely goodness and love will follow me
>all the days of my life,
and I will dwell in the house of the LORD
>forever.

What a promise! What a treasure. Because the Lord is our shepherd, we will lack no good thing. He will provide a sweet place of rest, a place to pull away from the stresses of life so that we may be found clothed and in our right mind. He will guide us on a righteous path, for surely left to ourselves we would be lost. Even in the darkest night, evil will hold no terror for us. There will be evil, but God will walk us through it. It will be clear to all who watch our lives, friend or foe, that the Lord provides for us.

"You anoint my head with oil; my cup overflows." It was a custom in the East to welcome guests with two offerings. First, the host would anoint his guest's head with a sweet perfume to display love and respect, and then he would give the guest a cup and fill it with an excellent wine until the wine ran over the edge. The message in Psalm 23 is that there is no shortage; Jesus has more than you could ever need.

Whatever you face today, remember that you walk by the side of the Shepherd, and he is committed to your care both now and forever.

In the process of writing I have been amazed by the path that Christ left for us. It is a marvelous thing to study the way he lived and the way he loved. There is no one like God. God is not like your pastor or husband, mother or father or friend. We have no reference point on this earth apart from Jesus. Let's take a fresh look at our God as revealed in the devotion of his only Son, our Savior. Jesus said that all that really matters is to love God with everything we have and are, and he showed us exactly how to do it.

For to us a child is born,

to us a son is given,

and the government will be on his shoulders.

And he will be called

Wonderful Counselor, Mighty God,

Everlasting Father, Prince of Peace.

ISAIAH 9:6

O little town of Bethlehem, how still we see thee lie!

Above thy deep and dreamless sleep the silent stars go by.

Yet in thy dark streets shineth the everlasting Light;

The hopes and fears of all the years are met in thee tonight.

PHILLIPS BROOKS

See, from His head, His hands, His feet,

Sorrow and love flow mingled down;

Did e'er such love and sorrow meet,

Or thorns compose so rich a crown?

ISAAC WATTS

CHAPTER FIVE

THE PRINCE OF PEACE

Keeping Our Eyes on Jesus

I slipped into my seat just as the lights were going down. I hugged my sister, Frances, who had saved a seat for me. My nephews, David and John, were taking part in this evening's nativity play. I hadn't seen them for some time, as they live in Scotland, and my home at that moment was in Southern California, but I was home for Christmas and made it in time for this evening's performance.

The lights came up on a hillside made of cardboard boxes and green felt. Six shepherds sat around an orange sixty-watt-bulb fire. They were suitably attired in their bathrobes and had dishcloths on their heads, held in place with rubber bands. One little shepherd kept wiggling his forehead, making his headgear fly off into space. The other shepherds found this extremely funny, as did most of the audience.

I spotted John in a familiar bathrobe. He was dragging a stuffed lamb on a string behind him. Our eyes met, and he shouted, "Hello, Aunt Sheila!" I waved at him, trying to stifle my laughter, because I knew if it escaped, it would only encourage further deviations from the script. But it was too late. He began a one-man show. He became the rebel shepherd whose story is not found in any of the gospel records. He swung the lamb over his head, round and round, until the string broke and the lamb was catapulted into the audience, assaulting an unsuspecting grandma.

Many of us have stories of the sweet, funny things that children have done as they attempted to portray the most inconceivable night on earth, the night when God became an eight- or nine-pound baby whose first human cry rang out in the cold air on a winter evening. I smile when we sing the line from the Christmas carol "Away in a Manger" that "little Lord Jesus no crying He makes." I imagine the writer felt compelled to separate this baby from every other baby who had ever been born, but it's hard to gloss over the reality of the Christ child's entrance onto our human stage.

A teenage girl became pregnant in a small town. That was scandalous! It put her in a class of women frowned upon by religious people. Never has such a miracle been so perfectly disguised. An angel had visited her and told her that the baby would be conceived by the Holy Spirit, but try telling that to scornful ears and skeptical hearts. Her cousin Elizabeth believed her, because she, too, was the recipient of a miraculous divine intervention. God gave Elizabeth and Zechariah a child when everyone around knew that they could not have children. All of Elizabeth's relatives and friends celebrated this glorious miracle. She was able to have her baby (who grew up to be John the Baptist) in her own home with the help of a midwife, surrounded by those she loved, but how different young Mary's experiences must have been. She spent the last few days of her pregnancy being bumped around on the back of a donkey, far away from home, and with no hotel reservation, no female help, and no mother's reassuring words.

We read the account of the trip from Nazareth to Bethlehem in Luke's gospel. Luke does not say how long in advance of Jesus' birth that Joseph left for Bethlehem or why he took Mary with him. As the head of the household, he could have gone alone. Perhaps Joseph didn't want to leave her in the company of wagging tongues. He may have used the emperor's order to travel to the town of one's birth to participate in a census (an enrollment before taxation) as a means of removing Mary from the stress of village gossip.

The English apologist Malcolm Muggeridge, in his book *Jesus: The Man Who Lives,* imagined what it would have been like if Mary had become pregnant with the Christ child in our time. "Mary's pregnancy, in poor circumstances, and with the father unknown, would have been an obvious case for an abortion; and her talk of having conceived as a result of the intervention of the Holy Ghost would have pointed to the need for psychiatric treatment and made the case for terminating her pregnancy even stronger. Thus our generation, needing a Savior more, perhaps, than any that has ever existed, would be too humane to allow one to be born."

Despite her culture and all the misunderstanding that would be heaped upon fragile shoulders, Mary said yes to God. "My soul glorifies the Lord and my spirit rejoices in God my Savior," she proclaimed, "for he has been mindful of the humble state of his servant. From now on all generations will call me blessed, for the Mighty One has done great things for me—holy is his name" (Luke 1:46-49). She welcomed the will of God to be played out in her life. She was just a girl, but more than that, she was a servant, a servant of the Most High God.

But before Mary said yes to God, God said yes to her. He said yes to you and to me. Mary needed a Savior, and she was given the privilege of carrying him before he would carry her.

It is still inconceivable to me that the magnificent God of the universe would allow his own Son to grow inside the womb of a young girl, to be spilled onto straw and hay, held by a man whose hands were cut and worn from fashioning wood, and nurtured by an uneducated teenage girl. That's how passionately God loves us.

I think we become so familiar with the Christmas story that we romanticize the reality of the enormous, outrageous gift that was placed into human hands and make the first morning when God opened his eyes on earth into something other than it was. It wasn't the pretty, sanitized stable of Christmas cards and nativity scenes. Jesus came to the poor in spirit and poor in the eyes of the world, exchanging the glory of angel worship for the smell of hay, the warm breath of animals, and the adoring eyes of a young virgin.

"Keep your eyes on Jesus," the apostle Paul wrote, "who both began and finished this race we're in. Study how he did it. Because he never lost sight of where he was headed—that exhilarating finish in and with God—he could put up with anything along the way: cross, shame, whatever. And now he's there, in the place of honor, right alongside God" (Hebrews 12:2, MSG).

I love that! If Jesus was going to show us how to live, he was going to live among us and show us step by step, day by day, and temptation by temptation all that really matters. So let's look at Jesus—the physical embodiment of one who loved God with heart, soul, mind, and strength and loved his neighbor as himself—and study how he lived. Our problems may be different, but this one thing is true: Because he started and finished this race we are in, Jesus has left a clear path for us to follow. There is nothing, absolutely nothing, that you and I will face that Jesus has not already shown us how to live through.

GOD AS A BOY

We don't know much about Jesus' first thirty years on earth, but we are given glimpses of the overture of his life. When he was eight days old, he was circumcised, as was the Jewish requirement for all baby boys, and at that time he was given the name Jesus. A woman was considered unclean after the birth of a child. That continued until thirty-three days after the circumcision of her son. At the end of that time she would present an offering to the Lord and be ceremonially clean again. Luke's gospel tells us that Mary offered two birds as a sacrifice, an indication that they were a poor family. Law permitted the offering of two birds or a lamb. A wealthier family would have offered a lamb.

One of the commentaries I read stated that Mary did not bring a lamb, but everything within me cried out, "You are wrong!" Mary brought the Lamb of God with her, and then she took him home to raise him to be the greatest sacrifice of all. If you read the Gospels through, it becomes very clear that at every point in his life, until standing before the Roman governor who could have saved his life, Jesus is in disguise.

Luke also provides the only biblical account of Jesus' boyhood. Every year his parents went to Jerusalem with friends and relatives for the Passover feast. The story that Luke tells us takes place when Jesus was twelve years old. At the conclusion of the Feast of the Passover, the families began the trip home. Joseph thought that Jesus was with his mother. Mary assumed he was with his dad. One day into the return trip they discovered that he was not in their group at all. They immediately returned to Jerusalem, but it took another whole day to find their son.

Can you imagine their concern? Jerusalem was a large, bustling city, and to have a child lost for three days must have been terrifying. I wonder as a mother myself whether the knowledge of how special Jesus was comforted Mary or added to her fear.

Have I let God down?

Have we delivered this holy boy into the hands of his enemies?

Finally they found him in the temple with the biblical scholars of his day. He was asking questions and also providing answers that amazed them. At first Mary was overwhelmed by what she saw and heard, and then her mom genes kicked in, and she was distraught with Jesus for causing them so much anxiety. His reply is significant. It's the first record we have of Jesus' declaring his special relationship with God the Father. " 'Why were you searching for me?' he asked. 'Didn't you know I had to be in my Father's house?' " (Luke 2:49).

I find two things fascinating here. First, his question: "Why were you searching for me?" What else would parents do? Jesus knew that for two nights he had slept somewhere apart from his parents, and yet he questioned their concern and confusion. Was he saying, "Where else would I be but here?" Then he declared his filial knowledge. "Didn't you know I had to be in my Father's house?"

We know almost nothing about Joseph, Jesus' earthly father, but I wonder how those moments played out in his soul. Joseph could trace his family tree back to King David, but this son, Jesus, was there before the foundation of the earth! Jesus was his son, but he was not his son, and this boy must have been a mystery to his father.

That's all we know until Jesus began his public ministry when he was thirty years old. We don't have a beam into those eighteen years other than a declaration that he was obedient to his parents, and he grew in wisdom, stature, and favor with both God and people (Luke 2:52).

When Barry and I discovered that we were going to have a baby, our plans for our child's future would have filled several journals. When we learned it was a boy, our lives were colored blue, I dreamt in blue, and we shopped for blue. His cradle was prepared as if it were holy ground, and when we placed his tiny frame in it for the first time, we stood and wept. I discovered a fierce protective force within me as a new mother that I had never known before. I'm sure if a stray dog had attempted to hurt my son, I could have literally torn it limb from limb.

In stark contrast to what all human parents want for their children, God allowed his Son to be born into poverty, political upheaval, and the hands of Herod the Great. The Romans had appointed Herod king of the Jews forty years before the birth of Christ. Herod was an ambitious man who had amassed great power and influence and allowed no one to threaten him in any way. He was also a brutal man, a man familiar with the feel of blood on his hands. He'd had his wife Mariamne and her two sons executed on a whim. When he knew that his advanced age was whispering that his own end was near, he ordered that five others should be killed on the day that he died to ensure an appropriate level of grief in the land! God allowed his only Son to be born under that rule and in that political climate.

Herod died when Jesus was four years old but not before committing that infamous crime, the slaughter of the innocents. When Herod heard from traveling astrologers (those we know as "the Wise Men") that a "king" had been born, he asked the Magi to continue their search and, when they found the child, to report back to him so he could add his voice to the celebration. The Magi were warned by God in a dream not to return to Herod, however, and so they traveled back to their homes another way. When Herod realized that he had been disregarded, he ordered that every boy in Israel under the age of two be slaughtered.

Can you imagine the agony of that night? This passage that I have read over and over in the past suddenly makes me bend over in grief as I try to imagine having my infant snatched out of my arms and brutally murdered on the crazed whim of a human despot. The streets ran red with the blood of innocent children, their only crime being that they were baby boys and their tiny cries might someday become the voices that would threaten the rule of this brutally ambitious king.

It has never been an easy thing to love God. It has never been a free ticket out of pain and the reach that sin has into the homes of godly people. I know that many of the babies who were slaughtered that night must have been born into homes where the parents loved and honored God. We have always been called to love God, even when life makes no sense and all that is in us wants to cry out, "Why?" In the rest of this chapter we'll take a look at key moments in the earthly life of Christ, moments that show us how to live no matter what we are facing. I think of them as the three hills of Golgotha.

Golgotha in the wilderness
Golgotha in the garden
Golgotha on the cross

I find I become so familiar with the stories of Jesus' life that the reality of what took place on earthly soil becomes diluted by time and a mental assent to what I think I know. That's why I want us to walk with Jesus through the temptations in the wilderness, the bleak desperation of the Garden of Gethsemane, the mockery of a trial, and wait with him as he hung suspended on the brutal gallows, the Son of God disguised as a common criminal. We are painfully familiar with the vicious carnage on the hill of the final Golgotha, that day that church tradition refers to as Good Friday, but there were deaths before that day. Jesus died to taking an easy way out when he was tempted by the devil in the wilderness, and he died to letting the cup of the wrath of God pass from him in the Garden of Gethsemane. Each of those cruel and lonely moments has much to say to us. I passionately believe that if we will faithfully study the way Christ lived and died, we will be gifted with a map that will see us through whatever we are facing now or will face in the future.

GOLGOTHA IN THE WILDERNESS

Scripture picks up the story of Jesus' life again as he is baptized by his cousin John. "The moment he came out of the water, he saw the sky split open and God's Spirit, looking like a dove, come down on him. Along with the Spirit, a voice: 'You are my Son, chosen and marked by my love, pride of my life'" (Mark 1:10-11, MSG). Immediately after this declaration of devotion from his heavenly Father, "Jesus, full of the Holy Spirit, returned from the Jordan and was led by the Spirit in the desert, where for forty days he was tempted by the devil. He ate nothing during those days, and at the end of them he was hungry" (Luke 4:1).

Jesus was led into the wilderness with its blistering heat by day and cold winds at night not by Satan but by the Spirit of God. He was left there in the ring with the one whose hatred of him ran as hot as molten steel. The Christ was left alone to be prodded, tested, and tormented for forty days.

I remember the winter that I decided to fast and pray for twenty-one days. I set aside three weeks in January when I had no obligations to ask God to aid me in this spiritual discipline. A friend offered the use of her apartment in Spain, and as I was living in England at the time, it was just a one-hour flight to a warmer climate and a quiet place where I could seek God's face away from the television and telephone.

The first week was awful. My head ached, and I longed for a cup of coffee. The second week was a little easier, but I felt weak even as I focused on God and enjoyed a tangible sense of his presence. As I came to the end of the third week, I experienced deep hunger pangs and great weakness, and I was ready to end my fast. I cannot imagine facing a demented angel determined to thwart the plans of God when I was so weakened physically. But Jesus went toe-to-toe with Satan at the moment when he was most humanly vulnerable. There was nothing for miles, no food and no company save this formidable adversary.

Satan tested Jesus to see if he would "show his stuff" and then take the easy way out of his suffering. The only reason we know some of what happened during those forty days is that Jesus must have told his friends what occurred. He was the only one there. It's obviously important, then, that we understand the message of the desert temptations. In each one is a lesson for you and me.

It's tempting to assume that this time of intense trial and temptation was easier for Jesus because he knew who he was and recognized his enemy, but I believe that each test was a terrible altar where Jesus died to every easy way out offered to him. The three temptations that Jesus faced just as his public ministry was getting under way clearly showed how he was going to live out his days:

1. He was going to depend totally on God for all his needs.
2. He would not take the easy way out but would take God's way, no matter what the personal cost was.
3. He would consider obedience to be more important than signs and wonders.

The First Temptation

> The devil said to him, "If you are the Son of God, tell this stone to become bread." Jesus answered, "It is written: 'Man does not live on bread alone.'" (Luke 4:3-4)

Jesus was hungry. Physically he was empty, and it would be hard to endure the cold desert nights with no internal fuel to sustain him. But the gospel writers tell us two things: one, Jesus was empty of food, and two, he was full of the Spirit.

If I examine my own life and the way we live as a culture, the opposite is usually true; we are physically full and spiritually empty. There was nothing inherently evil about bread, but the underlying principle is that Jesus said no to providing for himself and acting apart from total dependence on God. He was quoting the words of Moses from a passage in Deuteronomy in which Moses was reminding the stubborn children of Israel of the ways God had taken care of them. "He humbled you, causing you to hunger and then feeding you with manna, which neither you nor your fathers had known, to teach you that man does not live on bread alone but on every word that comes from the mouth of the LORD" (Deuteronomy 8:3).

The children of Israel spent forty years in the wilderness and at every turn made the wrong choice, took the wrong direction, lost faith and hope. Jesus spent forty days in the wilderness and set a new pattern of how to live in a way that honored God. Jesus was showing how it was always supposed to be. The Israelites demanded bread, and most died in the wilderness, never seeing the Promised Land, but Jesus refused to grab the reins from God, demonstrating instead loving obedience and trust even unto death, opening the way to the Promised Land for all of us.

What does this story say to you and to me? How does it teach us to live? Chances are we won't be led out into a physical desert where we are literally starving, but perhaps you feel as if you're in a spiritual desert—a dry, bleak place where it seems you have been abandoned. What gnaws at you as your greatest need? Perhaps you are waiting for a life partner or a child or a better job or improved health. You want to follow God, but it seems as if he is not providing what you need when you need it. Are you tempted to take things into your own hands and try to fix them?

Even as I'm writing today at one of my favorite coffee spots, I stop for a moment to stretch, and someone says, "Hello." It's a musician friend I haven't seen in some time. We catch up a little with each other, and he asks me what I'm writing. I tell him, and he says, "That's where my sister is. She's been married four times, and the fourth marriage is over now too. She's looking for something. She loves God, but she's still looking for something."

Jesus told Satan that it's more important to obey and trust God than to meet our own crying needs. I have found that what I truly long for is found in God alone and not in the things I think I need, no matter how good they are. Satan was not tempting Jesus to turn rocks into a narcotic, where to say yes would clearly be sin. The temptation was commonplace, part of natural life. That's what made it so hard. That's what is hard for you and me. We long for things that are good, but Jesus showed us we need to long for God and his highest will even more.

In 2001 at the Women of Faith conferences, I asked the audience a question: "If Jesus walked into this arena tonight when everyone else had left and told you that he would meet your greatest need, what would you ask for?" In talking with women at the end of the evening, I heard various answers: a husband, a child, physical health, financial security, and many more. My contention is that whatever we would ask for would not be enough. Just as our greatest sin is not loving God, our greatest need is to fall in love with Jesus and be filled with a desire to love him and obey him in every moment of our lives. "Because your love is better than life, my lips will glorify you" (Psalm 63:3).

The Second Temptation

> The devil led him up to a high place and showed him in
> an instant all the kingdoms of the world. And he said to
> him, "I will give you all their authority and splendor,

> for it has been given to me, and I can give it to anyone
> I want to. So if you worship me, it will all be yours."
>   Jesus answered, "It is written: 'Worship the Lord
> your God and serve him only.'" (Luke 4:5-8)

Jesus' adversary moved from simply asking Jesus to perform a miracle to the true evil intent behind his presence: "Worship me." If Jesus had bowed his knee to Satan, even for a moment, even due to physical weakness, that would be understandable, but we would be lost. Jesus would no longer be the perfect, innocent sacrifice that the holiness of God required. Before he became our sacrifice, two goats were used on the annual Day of Atonement. One goat was killed as a sin offering, and the priest would lay his hands on the head of the other goat, "transferring" onto it the sins of the people. The cursed "scapegoat" would then be sent into the wilderness to die. This was symbolic of what Christ would ultimately do. His sacrifice would atone for our sins once and for all, and they would be so far removed that God would remember them no more. What Satan was offering Jesus in this second temptation was the world without the cross, the joy without the pain.

Interestingly, Jesus didn't contradict him. He didn't tell him that he didn't have that power. It's significant to note that the devil was giving Jesus the glossy magazine version of the world, the splendor and not the sin that pulsates just below the surface. Jesus saw through the gloss to our desperate need for a Savior. Our need for a Savior necessitated a sacrifice that he alone could make. He knew that the sacrifice necessitated suffering. He knew that what the Enemy offered was not the will of his Father. After his death and resurrection, Jesus reminded the two men he walked with on the road to Emmaus, "Did not the Christ have to suffer these things and then enter his glory?" (Luke 24:26). Jesus refused to take the easy way out, and he used the Word of God to defuse the words of the Evil One.

My son began kindergarten in the fall of 2002. I am grateful that

Barry and I are able to send him to a private Christian school. The headmaster reminded the parents at our orientation meeting, "Christian education combines two things that God feels passionately about: truth and children." As I write, Christian is in his second week, and already I have been challenged by the integrity of the education offered. Each week the children memorize one verse of Scripture. Christian's verse for this week is "For all have sinned and fall short of the glory of God" (Romans 3:23).

As we were driving home from school yesterday, he asked me about the meaning of that verse. "Is that a good thing, Mom?"

"What, darling?" I asked.

"To fall short of the glory of God," he clarified.

"Goodness, no! That means that we are all sinners and needed Jesus to save us," I replied.

He thought about that for a moment. "Does that mean I am a sinner?" he asked incredulously.

"Yes, Christian. You are a sinner."

"Are you a sinner?" he continued.

"I am."

He seemed bowled over by this, but the clincher for him was when he brought Mary Graham, the wonderful, godly president of Women of Faith, into the conversation.

"Is Mary Graham a sinner?" he asked in a hushed tone.

"Yes, she is," I said.

"Boy, we're in trouble!" he concluded.

I reassured him that was the whole point of Jesus' being the perfect sacrifice. Only he could save us.

By fifth grade in Christian's school, the students have committed all of Psalm 139 to memory so they will know that every human being is precious, created in the image of God, so loving and respecting one another is not an option; it is a command. I am joining my son in this spiritual discipline of committing God's Word to memory. We live in corrupt, confusing days, and I know that the only way to stand against the evil schemes of the devil is to have the Word of God buried deep inside. This temptation that was presented to Christ—an easy way out, the payoff without the pain of denying himself—will be presented to each of us in various ways. Jesus combated every approach of the Enemy with the Word of God. If we don't know the Word, it will be much easier for the Enemy to deceive us. I have talked with women who have been caught up in extramarital affairs because the pain of trying to work on their own marriages seemed greater than the excitement of something offered with no apparent strings. It never works. It's always a disaster. But the temptation is to take the easy way out.

"I have hidden your word in my heart," the psalmist wrote, "that I might not sin against you" (Psalm 119:11). Jesus combated temptation with the Word of God, and we can too.

The Third Temptation

> The devil led him to Jerusalem and had him stand on the highest point of the temple. "If you are the Son of God," he said, "throw yourself down from here. For it is written:
>
> " 'He will command his angels concerning you
>   to guard you carefully;
> they will lift you up in their hands,
>   so that you will not strike your foot against a stone.' "
>
> Jesus answered, "It says: 'Do not put the Lord your God to the test.' " (Luke 4:9-12)

In this temptation Satan misquoted a passage from Psalm 91. He omitted the words "to guard you in all your ways." Rabbinic tradition held that the Messiah would appear not in a stable as a baby but on top of the temple, the very place that the devil encouraged Jesus to jump from. He was prodding Jesus to prove his lordship. He was goading him into a display of the spectacular. Jesus said no; God is not to be put to the test.

It's interesting that each temptation took something that actually was already Christ's in God and twisted it into the ultimate act of disobedience and mistrust. Of course God meets our physical needs; he gives us our daily bread. Yes, the kingdoms of the world belong to Christ and will bow to his lordship, and one day he will make the most magnificent descent in all of human history when he returns in glory. But Christ does everything in his Father's will and in his time.

I wonder how tempting it must have been at times for Christ to show who he was. When he met skepticism among the religious people, was he tempted to "show them"? Whether he was or not, he refused to give in to the very thing that the human spirit cries for: physical proof, a demonstration of the spectacular that would lead to special standing in the eyes of others.

It seems in our Christian culture these days that we give in far more easily to that temptation. We are impressed with anyone who appears to have a healing ministry, as if that says something about them rather than about God. If we hear of a church that seems to be experiencing a supernatural visitation of God, we throng to that place, hoping that the sight of such manifestations will make it easier to love our husbands or wives, teach our children, endure our physical illnesses, survive our financial crises. But Scripture bears witness to the fact that the human heart remains the same even in the presence of the fantastic.

Think of the children of Israel who saw the Red Sea part with their own eyes, who saw food fall from heaven every morning, and yet they continued to rebel. Think of Judas, of Peter, who saw the dead raised and a sandwich become a banquet, and still they betrayed him, still they denied even knowing him.

Miracles don't change our hearts. Obedience to God does.

I talked recently with a young man who is a relatively new believer. "I've been a Christian for almost two years now," he said. "When I first gave my life to Christ, I could really feel his presence. I saw so many answers to prayer. It was miraculous. Now things have changed. I don't know what's wrong, but I just don't feel God's presence as much anymore."

I understand his confusion. We want to see things, to feel things; we want God to show up in some miraculous way so there is no way we could doubt him. I have met many people who wanted signs, something spectacular, miracles, prosperity, victory over every human ill, and when God did not show up according to their prescription, they were confused and at times disillusioned. Christ showed us by his life that what matters, all that really matters, is to love God by trusting him and obeying his will. We are not called to be those who wear our relationship with God as a badge that entitles us to a spiritual dog and pony show. We are called to be those who demonstrate their relationship with God through a humble heart and an obedient spirit.

My favorite book apart from the Bible is Fyodor Dostoevsky's *The Brothers Karamazov.* Dostoevsky often gladly squandered himself, pursuing pleasure through bouts of drinking and gambling. As he was on his way to a prison camp in Siberia, condemned to death by Czar Nicholas I, a sentence that was then commuted to prison camp, a woman pressed a New Testament into his hands. He was allowed to keep this book in prison, and he pored over every page, devouring each word. For ten years he lived in this strange crucible—a mix of the living Word of God and the worst types of criminals imaginable—and from this came some of the most brilliant books that have ever been written.

In *The Brothers Karamazov* we read of an intellectually gifted brother, Ivan, who has no faith in God, and a simple, devout brother, Alyosha, who cannot meet his brother's probing questions with illuminating answers but whose life itself shines with love. One of the most spiritually luminous moments in the story comes when Ivan shares a poem called "The Grand Inquisitor" with Alyosha. He tells his brother that he didn't really write it, he just thought it up and memorized it.

The poem is set in Spain in the sixteenth century. It is really a battle between this grand inquisitor, an old man of ninety, and a figure who is clearly a disguised Jesus. The inquisitor recognizes Jesus and has him thrown into prison. When he visits him there, we are given a version of the scene between Christ and Satan in the wilderness temptations. The grand inquisitor tells the Christ figure what a mistake he made in the desert by giving up the three things men crave: miracle, mystery, and authority. He taunts him with an astounding declaration that even the church has recognized his error and has put everything back as it should be. Christians, too, now seek out miracle, mystery, and authority above all else. So the inquisitor reasons that he will have to put the Christ figure to death one more time, but this time not for Satan's benefit but to ensure that Jesus doesn't get in the way of the work of the church!

Does this strike you as profoundly as it does me?

Jesus lived and died to show us once and for all that love is the way.

Love is the way.

Love is the way.

GOLGOTHA IN THE GARDEN

Going a little farther, he fell with his face to the ground
and prayed, "My Father, if it is possible, may this cup
be taken from me. Yet not as I will, but as you will."
(Matthew 26:39)

It was quiet in the garden. His enemies were coming but not yet. His friends were asleep, lulled into careless slumber by full stomachs and sweet wine. He was alone. He didn't want to be alone tonight. What lay ahead of him was unspeakable, unimaginable, and the horror of the path that would lead out of the garden this night washed over him in sickening waves.

He thought back to his forty-day trial in the desert, an encounter with a fallen angel, his archrival who had pushed, prodded, and taunted him to see if he was who he appeared to be. In that place of death, of cruel rocks and wasted land, he had been offered a way out of all that tonight would hold.

"I'll give it all to you, and it won't cost a thing," Satan had said as they surveyed kingdoms as far as the eye could see. "It's what you want, isn't it, the love of the people? I can do this for you. It'll be the crown without the cross. I'll give you the payoff without the pain."

He had said no! It was not an easy no, as some might imagine. The temptation had been real and potent. He had been weak, bone tired, and once again alone. But he had said no. In saying no to that offer he had said yes to this dark and lonely night.

He fell on his face, the very earth that he had spoken into existence now mingling with the sweat that poured down his face. He thought of Lazarus, the final casualty he had encountered before this night. He had been filled with rage to see the devastation that ran like blood over the earth. This was not the once beautiful place his Father had created. The earth was now a place of broken bodies, broken hearts, and broken dreams, and the only way to reverse this hellish plot was for the Innocent of God, the Lamb as white as snow, to absorb all the evil that was tearing people's hearts and souls in two. This night would be the beginning of the greatest loneliness in heaven or on earth. There would be a moment when no one would be able to look at him, not even his Father. In that moment he would become everything that was corrupt and vile and hostile and wear it like a festering overcoat of shame, because there was no other way. There is no other way. There never will be another way.

I had the privilege of returning to school in 1993. I enrolled as a student at Fuller Theological Seminary to pursue a master's degree in theology. A professor who is an accomplished student of Mark's gospel taught one of my New Testament classes. He has made this gospel his area of expertise, and his enthusiasm over the content and pacing of the story Mark tells was very contagious and has stayed with me. It's a fascinating gospel to read in one sitting. I highly recommend it. There is a sense of urgency and dramatic storytelling when Mark brings us to the final days of Christ's life. At the beginning of chapter 14 he locks everything down into a tight countdown of the final hours. "Now the Passover and the Feast of Unleavened Bread were only two days away, and the chief priests and the teachers of the law were looking for some sly way to arrest Jesus and kill him" (Mark 14:1).

The importance of the passion and resurrection of our Lord for the early church is evidenced by the large amount of textual space the story takes in each of the four gospels, but especially in Mark's. The *New International Bible* commentary tells us that out of the 661 verses in Mark's gospel, 128 are devoted to the passion and resurrection story, and a total of 242 are devoted to Jesus' last week (from the Triumphal Entry to the Resurrection).

On the morning of the Golgotha in the garden, Jesus prepared to share one final meal with his closest friends who asked him, "Where do you want us to go and make preparations for you to eat the Passover?" (Mark 14:12). It was Thursday. Jesus and his disciples were most likely in Bethany that day, but since the Passover had to be eaten within the walls of the city of Jerusalem, time was at a premium. The Passover meal had to be eaten between sundown and midnight. Knowing what was just ahead, Jesus sat down with his friends to remember the time when God's people as hostages in Egypt splashed blood on the doorposts of their homes so they would be spared when the Lord passed over. Judas sat there with the other eleven disciples, knowing that he was just a few hours away from delivering Jesus to those who would spill his blood over everything. Then it was time. They sang one hymn, which traditionally was one of the psalms between Psalms 114 and 118. Jesus would have sung the lines, and the disciples would have responded with, "Hallelujah!"

Then they left for the Garden of Gethsemane. The garden is in the valley between Jerusalem and the Mount of Olives. Since Judas had slipped away by this point, Jesus asked eight of the disciples to wait at the entrance to the garden, and he asked Peter, James, and John—his three closest friends on earth—to come with him and share this nightmarish vigil. He walked a little ahead and fell on his face in an anguish of mind and soul that I cannot comprehend. "Abba, Father," Jesus prayed, "everything is possible for you. Take this cup from me. Yet not what I will, but what you will" (Mark 14:36).

What was the cup Christ was referring to?

"In the hand of the LORD is a cup full of foaming wine mixed with spices; he pours it out, and all the wicked of the earth drink it down to its very dregs" (Psalm 75:8).

All of hell was in that cup. All the evil that has played out on our planet—the treachery, murder, abuse, hatred, and desolation of a world in rebellion against God—was represented in that cup of suffering.

Even in this agony of body and mind, Jesus wanted the Father's will. "Yet not what I will, but what you will" (Mark 14:36). So he prayed and submitted to what God wanted.

Walter Wangerin Jr., in his wonderful book *Reliving the Passion,* comments that in the garden that night the Lord's Prayer was being acted out.

"Deliver us from evil" became "Let this cup pass from me."

"Thy will be done on earth as it is in heaven" became "Not my will but your will be done."

"Our Father in heaven" became a primal wail of "Abba, Father!"

When Jesus went back to his friends, they were fast asleep, slumped against the trunk of a tree. He was truly alone on this dreadful night.

"Could you men not keep watch with me for one hour?" he pleaded (Matthew 26:40). Can you hear the human cry in Jesus' words? "Just one hour—that's all I'm asking. I'm about to be slaughtered for you. Can't you give me one hour? You are my best friends in the world. Be with me now. I need you."

He went back to pray a second time, and when he returned, they were asleep again. This time he didn't bother to wake them. He went back to this garden Golgotha one more time to pray and left knowing that his Father was willing to let him carry the sin of the world.

Jesus' trial was a farce. As we saw in chapter 2, Jesus' condemnation came in two parts: a religious trial and a civil trial. During the religious trial, the high priest and religious leaders scavenged to find anything that would condemn Jesus. First he was brought before Annas, the former high priest and father-in-law to Caiaphas, the current high priest who was hellbent on Christ's destruction. Caiaphas sat in judgment, robed in scarlet, smug in his power as Jesus stood before him bound by ropes. They brought in witnesses, false witnesses whose stories canceled out one another. According to Old Testament law, to condemn a man to death required two witnesses, but they had to agree. "Anyone who kills a person is to be put to death as a murderer only on the testimony of witnesses. But no one is to be put to death on the testimony of only one witness" (Numbers 35:30).

Caiaphas was furious. Rising to his feet, he demanded that Jesus answer his accusers. Jesus said nothing. Finally the high priest posed the question that would save us all and condemn Jesus totally: "Are you the Christ, the Son of the Blessed One?" (Mark 14:61). I imagine they all held their breaths, perhaps some snickering at the absurdity of the question. Would he condemn himself now?

"I am," said Jesus.

Now he said yes when it would cost him everything. Now he said yes when to say nothing might save him. That's all it took. With dramatic flair Caiaphas ripped his robes, grateful that he no longer needed his useless witnesses as all in the room had heard Jesus' blasphemous assertion. To a man they rendered him guilty. Not content with that, they proceeded to attempt to humiliate him. They tied a blindfold around his eyes, and one after another punched him, taunting him to identify his assailants if he truly was a prophet. Then he was given over to the guards, who beat him.

By the early hours of Friday morning the chief priests, scribes, and elders had come up with their plan. They decided to accuse Jesus before a civil court but not of blasphemy, for in a civil court that would carry no weight, but of high treason, a crime punishable by death. This was the very thing that so many of Jesus' followers longed for, an uprising against the Roman powers by the Messiah, but Jesus had always refused. Now he stood condemned of that very crime.

The Roman governor's official residence was in Caesarea, on the Mediterranean coast, but when Pilate was in Jerusalem, he occupied Herod's palace. Finally the Christ child was brought into Herod's palace. This Herod, known as Herod Antipas, was the son of Herod the Great, who had slaughtered so many innocent Jewish boys in fear that one of them would prove a threat to his throne.

Pilate was apprised of the charges against Jesus before he was brought in. "And they began to accuse him, saying, "We have found this man subverting our nation. He opposes payment of taxes to Caesar and claims to be Christ, a king" (Luke 23:2).

I find it interesting to note here the assault on all fronts of a Father and his Son by two fathers and their sons. On the religious front there is Annas and his son-in-law Caiaphas, and on the civil front, Herod the Great and Herod Antipas. Herod the Great had tried to destroy Christ, and now in the palace of his son the death sentence would be issued. They did not know that God the Father and Jesus the Son had divinely planned to let them win in this small arena so that all who would come home to the Father through the Son could be free—even Annas and Caiaphas, even Pilate and Herod, if they would bow to the only true King they would ever encounter.

Pilate didn't want to condemn this man, so he offered to release him under the Passover provision of releasing one prisoner. The crowd screamed for the release of Barabbas, a man who had been imprisoned for insurrection against the Roman government. It is thought that his name was probably Jesus Barabbas, so when the crowd called for his release, Pilate may well have mistaken which Jesus they were referring to, but there was to be no doubt that day who would hang on the cross. The chief priests moved through the crowd like a lethal virus, stirring up hatred and a lust for blood. Accepting that the crowd wanted Barabbas to be released, Pilate then asked a strange question. "What shall I do, then," he asked them, "with the one you call the king of the Jews?" (Mark 15:12).

How strange for the Roman governor to ask a brawling crowd what should happen to a prisoner, but sentiment was running high, and hatred poured out of every corner, every face, and every raised voice like a river of poison ready to consume anyone who stood in its way. Pilate stood on the edge of a razor. On one side was a vicious crowd crying for blood—not just any blood but Lamb's blood; on the other was his certainty that this was an innocent man. His wife's words were ringing in his mind like the warning bell on an ocean buoy. "Don't have anything to do with that innocent man, for I have suffered a great deal today in a dream because of him" (Matthew 27:19). Heaven and hell stood in silent horror and anticipation. Again and again Pilate questioned Jesus and returned to the crowd saying he found no offense. But there was to be no appeasement that day.

Finally, in bitter resignation, Pilate performed a peculiarly Jewish habit, described in Deuteronomy 21:6-7. "Then all the elders of the town nearest the body shall wash their hands over the heifer whose neck was broken in the valley, and they shall declare: 'Our hands did not shed this blood, nor did our eyes see it done.' " Perhaps in mockery of all that the religious people stood for, Pilate washed his hands in front of the crowd and delivered Jesus into the pit of hellish hatred before him.

GOLGOTHA ON THE CROSS

> For you know the grace of our Lord Jesus Christ, that
> though he was rich, yet for your sakes he became poor,
> so that you through his poverty might become rich.
> (2 Corinthians 8:9)

They took him from Pilate, and it was not enough to know that he would never lay his head down another night on this earth as a man. They had to beat him, flail him, tear his back in shreds, and drive a ring of thorns into his scalp. They pretended to worship; they laughed and spat in his face. Now Christ was silent; he didn't say a word. They forced the crossbeam of his own gibbet onto his broken, bleeding back and dragged him through the crowd. It was the custom of men condemned to be crucified to carry their own crossbeam, but it was not the custom to beat them almost to death beforehand.

Jesus stumbled from exhaustion and loss of blood. The hooks on the leather whip had shredded flesh and muscle. Impatient with his progress, perhaps afraid of the crowd and the rage that washed over them in waves, the guards grabbed a man named Simon from the crowd to carry the cross. Simon, a Jew, was no doubt on his way to celebrate the Passover. He was on his way to thank God for showing mercy in Egypt. Little did he know that he was carrying the cross of the One who would lay his body down to show mercy to us all.

As Jesus arrived at Skull Hill, someone rushed forward with a sponge soaked with myrrh. Myrrh was a mild narcotic, a painkiller. Jesus said, "No." He was already drinking. He was drinking from the cup of the wrath of God. Walter Wangerin Jr. writes in *The Passion Relived,* "What has the Lord been doing since Gethsemane? Drinking. Not from the woman's narcotic cup but from the cup the Father would not remove from him: drinking."

Suddenly the sky turned as black as night. Rain began to fall, heavy and frightening; thunder roared, as if all of heaven were crying out in pain; lightning tore the sky in two. Did God want to rip the earth apart and throw it away for what it had cost him on this day? Three hours— from noon till three. Three hours of hellish noise. Then silence for a moment.

"Eloi, Eloi, lama sabachthani?"

"My God, my God, why have you forsaken me?" (Matthew 27:46).

We will never know the depth of that agonizing cry as Jesus tasted the very core of hell: complete separation from God. John's gospel tells us that Jesus' last words were "It is finished" (John 19:30). The words for "Jesus said" in the Greek text—*phone megale*—translate as "megaphone." This expression is almost certainly a shout of victory—the greatest cry of triumph this earth will ever hear. Jesus was saying, "I've done it! Death has no sting, and hell has been forever plundered!"

After Jesus' death we are introduced to a brave man, Joseph of Arimathea. He was a prominent citizen, a member of the Sanhedrin (the supreme court of the Jews), who went to Pilate and asked for the body of Jesus. Who would have wanted to encounter Pilate again on that day? He had been warned by his wife to leave Christ alone. He had sat in the palace as the sky turned black. He would be in no mood to grant a favor. At first he refused to believe that Jesus was dead. Pilate knew that it usually took a man three days to die on a cross. Joseph persisted. He assured him that Jesus was dead. Pilate called for the centurion who had watched at the foot of the cross. The centurion confirmed that Jesus was dead, so Pilate agreed to let Joseph have the body.

This was highly unusual, as a body should have been released only to a family member when the charge was high treason. Mary was too distraught, and there is no mention of any other family member being there. Pilate's release of the body to Joseph seems further proof that he never believed Christ to be guilty in the first place.

I wonder at that scene on the hill. Joseph would have rested a ladder against the back of the cross. The two men on either side of Christ were no doubt still alive. Joseph would have had to tie a rope around Christ's chest to hold him up as he then pulled the spikes from his wrists. He would have climbed down, pulled the spike from his ankles, and lowered the body onto a clean white sheet, a shroud. Joseph was a wealthy man; he must have had servants to help him as he prepared Christ for burial.

Jesus' body was placed on a shelf in a cave carved into the rock, and a heavy stone was rolled in place at the entrance. Saturday passed. The Sabbath was over at six in the evening, but it would have been too dark to go to the tomb at that time of night, so the three women who had stood vigil at Golgotha waited till the early hours of Sunday morning to anoint Christ's body. This was not an embalming ritual, as the Jews didn't practice that. It was simply an act of love.

As they were walking to the cemetery, perhaps all they could talk about was how on earth they would budge the stone. Imagine their shock when they arrived and saw the stone had been rolled away. They must have been terrified, but they looked into the tomb. There was a man inside, sitting up. I'm sure they screamed, for he said to them, "Don't be alarmed.... You are looking for Jesus the Nazarene, who was crucified. He has risen! He is not here" (Mark 16:6).

Those three words have changed our lives! *He is risen.* Because Jesus not only died but also rose from the dead, there is nothing that we will face alone. There is nothing that today or tomorrow will bring that we can't face, because he is with us and has left a path for us to follow.

My premise in this chapter has been the firm belief that if we will study the life of Christ, we will begin to understand this simple plan he has left for us. At every twist and turn of the road Jesus put flesh on what it looks like to love God with heart, soul, mind, and strength and to love one's neighbor as oneself. In the desert, in the garden, and on the cross Jesus showed us the way. Now how do we live out his plan in our own lives?

You can know the law by heart without knowing the heart of it.

PHILIP YANCEY

Above all else, guard your heart,

for it is the wellspring of life.

PROVERBS 4:23

Oh, be generous in your self-surrender!

Meet His measureless devotion for you,

with a measureless devotion to Him.

Be glad and eager to throw yourself headlong into His dear arms,

and to hand over the reins of government to him.

HANNAH WHITALL SMITH

CHAPTER SIX

WHOLEHEARTED DEVOTION

Loving God with All Our Heart and Soul

It was a Saturday afternoon, and Barry, Christian, and I were driving past the mall on our way home from a myriad of weekend errands.

"Mom, look!" Christian cried out with excitement in his voice. "Over there. Over there!"

I looked to see what had fired him up. Two minutes before this exuberant announcement he had told his dad and me that if we did one more thing, he would expire. I looked, and there in the parking lot of the mall I saw what had reinflated his balloon. It was a carnival. It wasn't a huge affair. It was the kind that travels from city to city, stays for a few days, and moves on.

"Can we go? Can we go? Please, please, pleasy please."

Barry and I laughed as we changed lanes and pulled into the parking lot. We were instantly engulfed in the usual aromas: cotton candy, hot dogs, and funnel cakes mixed in with the oil and grease that keep the rides running. Barry does not do rides, so he usually ends up holding all our stuff as Christian and I hop from the Ferris wheel to the spinning spider to the mini–roller coaster. Where Barry shines is in the sideshows. He throws a mean dart, shoots ducks that never stood a chance out of the water, and can guess the weight of the man who looks as if he spends his life going from the hot dog stand to the funnel cakes and back again. By the end of the evening, we had won seven stuffed animals, two glow-in-the-dark swords, a 3-D picture of Spider-Man, and two fish. Christian took some time over the naming ceremony, finally settling on Smiler and Scaredy Fish.

After his bath that night, Christian assembled all the new furry creatures by his bed before he said his prayers. "Dear God, thank you for a cool day. Thank you for my new toys and the fish. Now about the fish, can you help me here? I have no luck with fish. Amen."

I empathized with his prayer, making a mental note to discuss the idea of "luck" with him when he might be more receptive. We have flushed a lot of fish in our family—betta, angelfish, rainbow fish, and enough goldfish to feed a posse of stray cats. Our fish usually last one day, and then Christian will make the announcement that we have another floater. At first it was distressing to him, and we buried the first two or three in the yard with the appropriate pomp and ceremony, but it can be emotionally exhausting getting oneself geared up for yet another fish funeral. Now, with a few simple, kind words, we flush them. Christian usually calls after them, "Return to the sea!"

The next morning Christian checked to see if our two new friends were alive and kicking and was relieved to observe that they had made it through the long, dark night.

"I love these fish," he declared.

"Me, too," I agreed. "As fish go, these two are splendid specimens."

"No, they're goldfish," he informed me, then turned to me with his big brown eyes. "How much do you love me, Mom?"

"I love you more than all the stars in the sky, the sand on all the beaches in the world…"

He was not looking impressed. I tried again.

"I love you more than all the Starbucks in America!"

"Wow!" he said. That was big.

"I love you more than God," he said.

"I know you love me, Sweet Pea, but no one loves more than God."

"I do," he answered. "Don't you love me more than God, Mom?"

What a question. We sat and talked for a while about what it means to love God and our family, that all love comes from God and it's a gift.

"Well," he said. "The Bible tells me to love God more, but my heart tells me to love you more."

I understand that sentiment from a five-year-old child. It's appropriate. It would be a rare young child who knew enough about the greatness of God to depend more on him than on his or her parents. But what about when we're all grown up? What if you are single, and even as you thank God for his eternal embrace, you long to have human arms around you too? If you had to choose, would there be times when it would be a tug of war? Perhaps God has gifted you with a husband and children, and you know that if anything happened to them, you would be furious with God.

God has created us with a desire for relationship; it is part of the gift of being human. Think of the human walk of Jesus Christ. He chose twelve men to be his friends. He had three best friends. He knew what it was to be lonely, misunderstood, overlooked; he longed for companionship in the Garden of Gethsemane, someone to share the grief and horror of the day to come. He honored his mother but made it clear that he had his Father's business to do. Jesus modeled loving relationships fueled by a heart passionate for the will of God to be done in his life.

So what does it mean to love God with all of our heart and soul? When I think of loving that way, I think of absolute, wholehearted devotion: recognizing who God is, that he is Lord above all, that he is good and kind, that he is worth everything we could ever offer. In this chapter I have paired heart and soul together, just as they are often paired in Scripture.

> You know with all your heart and soul that not one of
> all the good promises the LORD your God gave you has
> failed. (Joshua 23:14)

> Now devote your heart and soul to seeking the LORD
> your God. (1 Chronicles 22:19)

> They entered into a covenant to seek the LORD, the
> God of their fathers, with all their heart and soul.
> (2 Chronicles 15:12)

I want to look at two unusual characters and see what we can learn from them that can inform our relationship with God. They are Ruth and Bulka. We are familiar with Ruth from the book of Ruth in the Old Testament. Bulka was devoted to the Russian writer Leo Tolstoy. Bulka was Tolstoy's dog!

RUTH

I'll begin with Ruth. Then hopefully I can talk you into considering the dog! Ruth's story begins in the days when the judges ruled the people of God. We know from church history and from the book of Judges that it was a time of lawlessness and chaos in Israel (Judges 21:25). It was the responsibility of the judges to function as military leaders in time of war; they also served as local rulers, dispensing political and legal justice. It was a time not only of disorder but also famine, which must have added to the unrest. They were dependent on rainfall at the right time, and if it failed, crops failed too, and everyone suffered. In God's providence it was this drought that caused Ruth to meet her first husband, Mahlon, and his family.

Bethlehem is about six miles south of Jerusalem. The name Bethlehem means "house of bread," because the region was very fertile, but the famine was so widespread that Naomi and Elimelech, Ruth's future in-laws, had to move out of their region to find food. They went to Moab, just east of the Dead Sea. After they had settled there, Elimelech, the head of the family, died, leaving his wife, Naomi, with two sons. The two boys married women from Moab, Ruth and Orpah. (That's Orpah, not Oprah!) Ten years later both sons died, so now there were three widows with no means of supporting themselves.

Naomi heard from someone that there was food again in Judah, so they packed up all they could take with them and headed for Naomi's homeland. It seems from the story that before they got very far, Naomi realized there wouldn't be much of a life for the girls there. Ruth and Orpah would be leaving all that they knew and going to a strange land where Naomi had no more sons for them to marry. She noted sarcastically that even if by some miracle she got pregnant and had two more sons, it would be quite some time before they were of marrying age.

She must have been a remarkable woman, however, because the girls were determined to stay with her. Naomi encouraged them to go back and find husbands and have children of their own. She pointed out how much bleaker her situation was than theirs. She seems to have interpreted losing her sons and her husband as God's anger toward her. Naomi would be returning to her people but no longer as a mother and wife. The Israelites believed that if life went well with you, it was because God was pleased with you; if tragedy struck, it was God's judgment on you. Naomi's conviction was that she was returning alone, poor, and with the mark of God's displeasure for all to see. She expressed the hope that her daughters-in-law would find "rest" by finding new husbands. This word *rest* refers to the social and financial security that marriage gave a woman in that time and culture. Naomi's situation must have seemed wretched to her, as she would be totally at the mercy of others' charity.

Orpah agreed to go back to Moab, and weeping bitterly she kissed her mother-in-law good-bye. Ruth refused to go, and we are given that beautiful declaration of wholehearted devotion from Ruth to Naomi, which I love to read in the *King James Version* of the Bible: "Entreat me not to leave thee, or to return from following after thee: for whither thou goest, I will go; and where thou lodgest, I will lodge: thy people shall be my people, and thy God my God: Where thou diest, will I die, and there will I be buried: the LORD do so to me, and more also, if ought but death part thee and me" (Ruth 1:16-17).

What a beautiful example of a woman's total commitment to loving and serving another even unto death. What a wholehearted pledge.

Whatever happens to you happens to me.

Whomever you love, I will love.

Wherever you die, I will die there too.

This was a sold-out lifelong vow. Ruth didn't say that she would go with Naomi until the older woman died and then return home; she made it clear that Naomi's people were now her people and Naomi's God was now her God. I think loving with all our heart and soul must look like that. If you read the rest of her story, you will see that God had wonderful things in store for Ruth when she and Naomi reached Bethlehem, but Ruth didn't know that when she made her pledge of loyalty.

When the women arrived home, the townspeople were in a tizzy. The commotion caused by Naomi's return may have been from the joy of seeing her again, or it may have resulted from her friends' shocked whispering about her abject, changed appearance. "Can this be Naomi?" the townswomen wondered (Ruth 1:19). Naomi was home, but she was returning in sorrow. She asked that no one call her Naomi, which means "pleasant," but rather Mara, which means "bitter." "I went away full, but the LORD has brought me back empty," she said. "Why call me Naomi? The LORD has afflicted me; the Almighty has brought misfortune upon me" (Ruth 1:21).

The one bright star on Naomi's horizon was Ruth. Ruth was determined to honor her commitment to her mother-in law and set out to find a way to feed herself and Naomi. She began the common practice of gleaning in the fields, walking behind others as they harvested the grain so she could gather up what they dropped. It wasn't long before she caught the eye of the owner of the field, Boaz, who happened to be a distant cousin of Naomi's husband. He welcomed Ruth and told her to keep gathering food in his field and that he would make sure his men didn't bother her. He had heard of Ruth's unusual loyalty to her mother-in-law. He was taken with her.

Naomi was a wise woman and realized before Ruth did that Boaz had fallen for the young Moabitess. She advised Ruth that when evening came and Boaz was asleep on his threshing floor after a good meal, she should slip in and rest at his feet, raising the corner of the foot of his robe to cover her. Ruth did exactly as she was told. Some commentators have suggested that what Naomi told Ruth to do was wrong and sexual in nature, but if we consider that Boaz's mother was Rahab, a known prostitute back in Jericho who was spared by the grace of God, then it's unlikely Naomi would have pushed Ruth into an act that would have discredited her with Boaz. It was in fact a Hebrew custom for a widow to lie at a man's feet to make it clear that she was appealing for a proposal of marriage from him as her husband's next of kin.

Naomi's plan worked. Boaz was thrilled that, instead of trying to catch the eye of a younger man, she looked to him. They were married and had a son. They named him Obed, and he would later have a grandson named David. Because of Ruth's wholehearted devotion and the actions that sprang from her love, she became the great-grandmother of one of Israel's kings, and her name is recorded in Matthew's gospel as one who stands in the lineage of Jesus Christ.

We never know what God has in store when we love with all our heart, expecting nothing in return.

BULKA

Now what about Tolstoy's dog, Bulka? Tolstoy is a celebrated writer known for such literary classics as *War and Peace* and *Anna Karenina*. He was born to an aristocratic Russian family in 1828. His books are brilliant, even though he never completed a college education. From an early age he was familiar with sorrow. His mother died when he was two years old, and his father died when the boy was nine. When Tolstoy was twenty-three, he joined the army and went off to fight in the Crimean War. He was a man torn between heaven and earth, his love of land, words, and people, and a final repudiation of all of that. In 1910 he left his estate, his wife, and children and was found dead on a cot in a railway station. He had established a school for the children of peasants who were receiving no education, left magnificent books behind, but never found any peace for his own soul.

As well as his adult classics, he also wrote for children. I first read about Bulka, a small, stocky bulldog with a stubborn streak, in his book *Classic Tales and Fables for Children*. We meet Bulka as Tolstoy set off to join his brother in the army. Tolstoy knew he couldn't take his dog with him to the rigors of army life, so, recognizing the dog's passionate loyalty and devotion, he decided to leave while it was still dark. He gave orders that Bulka was to be chained up in the shed until he was safely on his way. He crept out of the house in the early hours of the morning and mounted his horse for the twelve-mile ride to his first posting station.

After arriving there, he was about to set off with a fresh horse when he saw something black speeding down the road like a hairy bullet. It was Bulka. He had broken his chain, jumped out of the window, and run twelve miles to find his master. He was exhausted and thirsty, but all he would do was wag his tail and lick his master's hand. It seems as if this faithful dog was one of the few who reached Tolstoy's heart.

A COMMON THREAD

You may find Ruth and Bulka a strange pairing, but a common thread runs through their stories—a passion and love that are single minded and utterly devoted. It's a heart-and-soul love that is rewarded. Ruth finds a husband and has a child whose blood will run in royalty. Bulka is sworn into the army with his master and follows Tolstoy to the Caucasus.

So the first thing I notice about a love that encompasses heart and soul is that it is a single-minded love, focused and wholehearted. There is a glorious freedom in being so sold-out rather than being torn in a multitude of different directions. That's how I want to love God. I want my love to be focused and true. Think how much simpler life would be if we loved God like that. Every decision would be filtered through that standard. There would be only one person to please, and in pleasing him we would be able to honor all our other relationships.

Mother Teresa was a mentor to everyone who came into contact with her. Her sold-out devotion to Christ was the hallmark of her life, and she constantly rebuffed any suggestion that she should be emulated in any way but for her love of Christ. A student was volunteering with the sisters one summer in Calcutta. Mother Teresa saw him sitting on a wall one morning, looking as if he was carrying the weight of the world. She asked him what was wrong.

"There are so many people to help. I want to serve them all, but where do I start?"

Mother Teresa replied, "Your call is to serve Christ. That is all, serve him only."

Perhaps you feel weighed down by the responsibilities in your life, by the number of demands placed on your time and energy every day. Our call is not to "fix" everyone else, please everyone else, or live up to everyone else's expectations of us. Our call is simply to wholeheartedly love Christ; then he will direct our steps.

A NEW HEART

Perhaps feeling overly responsible is not your problem. Rather you feel unable to give your whole heart because it seems so fragmented, damaged, unworthy of offering to Christ.

"I don't think I belong here," she whispered in my ear.

"Why don't you think you belong?" I asked the woman in my book line at a Women of Faith conference.

"I've only been a Christian for a couple of months, and I've done some stuff in my life that would make your hair curl," she replied.

I smiled, resisting my usual impulse to make a joke. She was too serious for that. Her eyes had the uncomfortable look of someone who suddenly realizes that she has shown up at the wrong wedding, she doesn't know anyone else in the room, and she had better get out quickly before anyone asks who she is.

"Anyway, would you sign my book?" she continued.

"You do belong here," I said. "Christianity is the one place where the only qualification is that you don't qualify."

She looked at me as if I were speaking in riddles. "What do you mean?" she asked.

"I don't know you," I said, "but I'm going to guess it's sexual stuff or drugs or alcohol that makes you believe you don't belong."

"Try all three!" she confirmed.

"All right then, let me repeat what I said: You belong here. Jesus doesn't judge you; he loves you. It doesn't matter what you've done because it can be forgiven—anything!"

She smiled at me and slipped away into the crowd. Later that day Ce Ce Winans sang her best-selling song "Alabaster Box." I prayed that the woman had stayed to hear it, for this was her story.

> Now one of the Pharisees invited Jesus to have dinner
> with him, so he went to the Pharisee's house and re-
> clined at the table. When a woman who had lived a
> sinful life in that town learned that Jesus was eating at
> the Pharisee's house, she brought an alabaster jar of per-
> fume, and as she stood behind him at his feet weeping,
> she began to wet his feet with her tears. Then she wiped

them with her hair, kissed them and poured perfume
on them. (Luke 7:36-38)

It's quite a scene. Jesus had accepted an invitation to a private dinner party at one of the Pharisees' homes. It was customary to allow the
poor and needy to visit at the end of such a meal to receive what was
left over, but this woman who slipped in didn't come to get something.
She came to give something. We are told that she lived a sinful life in
that town. What a picture that simple phrase conjures up. She was a
known sinner in a small town. Two thousand years have come and
gone, but some things never change. It must have taken a great deal of
courage for this woman to push through everyone's judgment and
make her way to Jesus.

She carried with her a small jar of very expensive perfume, and her
single-minded mission was to pour it over Jesus' feet. She didn't stand
in front of Jesus, but Luke tells us that she knelt behind Jesus, and
before she was able to open the jar, she soaked his feet with her tears,
dried them with her hair, and kissed them. Then she anointed his feet
with the sweet perfume.

Jesus' host, Simon, watched the interchange with a critical eye. The
Pharisee didn't outwardly challenge Jesus, but internally he thought
that if Jesus was indeed a prophet, he would know what kind of
woman this was. If he knew, then surely he would never let her touch
him. Since he didn't stop her, this was proof to Simon that Jesus was a
fraud. According to Luke, this monologue took place only in Simon's
head, but Jesus addressed him, answering the unspoken questions with
a question of his own.

"Two men owed money to a certain moneylender. One owed him
five hundred denarii, and the other fifty. Neither of them had the
money to pay him back, so he canceled the debts of both. Now which
of them will love him more?"

The Pharisee reluctantly answered him, "I suppose the one who had the bigger debt canceled." Jesus assured him that was the right answer (Luke 7:41-43).

Then Jesus turned to face the woman, but his comments were addressed to Simon. He looked the woman straight in the eye as he compared all that she had done for him to the religious man's lack of common courtesy.

> I came into your house. You did not give me any water for my feet, but she wet my feet with her tears and wiped them with her hair. You did not give me a kiss, but this woman, from the time I entered, has not stopped kissing my feet. You did not put oil on my head, but she has poured perfume on my feet. Therefore, I tell you, her many sins have been forgiven—for she loved much. But he who has been forgiven little loves little. (Luke 7:44-47)

Christ's behavior here is revolutionary. He honors a prostitute over a Pharisee. He values tears over expensive wine and repentance over rule keeping. The message is clear: It doesn't matter what you have done; all that matters is that you are repentant. Humility is precious to God.

But my heart is just too tarnished, you may think. *I have made so many bad choices that I no longer have anything worth offering to God.*

If you have messed up, if you are in the middle of the chaos of bad choices, there is a way home for you. If, like King David after he committed adultery with Bathsheba, you will ask God to forgive you, he will give you a new heart, a new beginning, a straight path, and he will never, never bring up your sin again. David prayed, "Have mercy on me, O God, according to your unfailing love; according to your great compassion blot out my transgressions. Wash away all my iniquity and cleanse me from my sin" (Psalm 51:1-2).

The Woman
Heart pounding in her ears, roaring waves of self-hatred
She takes the next step.
Shame pasted to her clothes, her story known, despised
She takes the next step.
At his feet, unable to stand, felled by beauty she had
        never known
She takes the next step.
Tears fall like pebbles, weighty, endless, a waterfall of regret
She takes the next step.
Hair that men have pulled, played with, spat at, now
        dry his feet
She takes the next step.
Perfume poured, all she had, all she knew, nothing now,
        a love offering
She takes the next step.
Eyes upon her, different eyes, eyes of love, rivers of
        mercy, a new day
She takes the next step.

Wherever you are, just take the next step.

WHITE AS SNOW

Beth Moore was a guest speaker at two of our conferences in 2002. I
was familiar with the popularity of her books and was eager to meet her.
She is a lovely woman, gifted, humble, and an ardent student of the
Word of God. As she spoke one Friday night, I was arrested by her honesty. Beth talked about sins wreaked upon her as a child and consequent
poor choices she made as an adult feeling trapped in an endless pattern
of recurring behavior. No one in the arena that night left doubting that
regardless of how far or how often you have fallen, God's arms are

longer. But it was a visit that Beth made to The Cove, Dr. Billy Graham's retreat center, that stayed in my thoughts as I lay in bed that night.

Beth is loved and honored as an in-depth Bible teacher and was invited to speak there in that capacity. As she walked through the center, a tribute to the life and ministry of Dr. Graham, she told us that her overwhelming emotion was that she did not belong there. That would seem ridiculous to those who know and love her. She is a trophy of grace used powerfully in the lives of others, and yet still this sense of condemnation hounded her. She explained, "You have to admit he is a man who has made some very good choices in life. As I looked at every good choice Billy Graham had made, I thought, 'God, you are worth that!' " Beth said she felt ashamed, bereft—as if she were facing afresh just how dishonoring some of her choices had been to a God who deserved the very best his children could possibly offer.

I understood what she meant. God is worth getting it all right. Not that Dr. Graham has made perfect choices at every juncture of his life, but something deep inside us realizes that the more we know God, the more we understand that he is worth every sacrifice, every self-denial, and every rejection of sin. The wonderful thing about God, however, is that whether we have made two bad choices or two thousand bad choices, his message is the same:

I love you.

I forgive you.

I will wash you as white as snow.

God had a surprise in store for Beth the next morning. She woke up, looked out the window, and couldn't believe what she saw. She shouted for her friend Jan Silvious, who was staying with her, to come and look.

"Tell me what that is!" she said pointing to a tree. "Is it frost, or is it snow?"

"It's snow," Jan replied, smiling at the Texan's encounter with the white stuff.

Beth describes how she jumped up and down, crying out, "I'm white as snow! I'm white as snow!"

It was almost unheard of to have snow at that time of year in North Carolina, but it was a clear message to Beth, a telegram from God. The Lord's reassurance in Isaiah 1:18 rang in her heart: "Though your sins are like scarlet, they shall be as white as snow; though they are red as crimson, they shall be like wool."

Are you tormented by shadows from the past? God can set you free to lift up your face and see how much he loves you. The more we understand the deep, deep love of God, the more we respond with love to him.

In his book *Celebrating the Wrath of God*, Jim McGuiggan relates the story told by Russell Maltby of a man whose wife kept leaving him for another man only to return repentant time after time. The husband always took her back. His friends questioned the wisdom of his welcome, but he responded, "Not a word! She's my wife!" After one final return, she died in her husband's arms.

On hearing this story, a marriage counselor responded by saying that the husband's "psychological problems needed to be looked at." What do you think? His wife's behavior was very abusive. Few would question him if after several defections he refused to let his wife return home. But isn't that how God loves us? We fail time after time, and God never closes the door in our face.

I think God sometimes gives a person unusual grace for an impossible situation to show us a glimpse of what God's relentless, wholehearted love is like. Richard Foster in his book *Prayer* says, "The love of the Father is like a sudden rain shower that will pour forth when you least expect it, catching you up into wonder and praise and unspeakable speech. When this happens, do not put up an umbrella to protect yourself but rather stand in the drenching rain of the Father."

Rain on us, Father. Rain on us.

But even as we stand in the rain of the love of God, voices call to us through the mist—voices from our past, from our flesh, and from our culture. How do we fix our minds on Christ when we are seduced by the siren call of voices deep inside?

> Now I lay me down to sleep.
> I pray the Lord my mind to keep
> And give me peace and rest this night.
> Come fortress me, O Lord of light.

Test me, O LORD, and try me,

examine my heart and my mind;

for your love is ever before me,

and I walk continually in your truth.

PSALM 26:2-3

Do not conform any longer to the pattern of this world,

but be transformed by the renewing of your mind.

Then you will be able to test and approve

what God's will is—his good, pleasing and perfect will.

ROMANS 12:2

May the mind of Christ, my Savior

Live in me from day to day,

By His love and pow'r controlling

All I do and say.

KATE B. WILKINSON

CHAPTER SEVEN

I WILL FOLLOW YOU

Loving God with All Our Mind

A man decided to purchase a pet. He wanted to find something that would be a good companion but also fairly low maintenance. He looked at kittens and rejected them as he picked their fur off his coat. He looked at dogs, but they required walking, apparently every day. Fish seemed too impersonal. So he settled on a parrot. He told the pet store owner that he wanted one that would talk.

"I have just the bird for you, sir. This one is a great talker!"

The man took the bird home, set it up in its cage, and watched. Nothing. After a few days he went back to the store.

"The bird you sold me doesn't talk," he said.

"I'm very surprised," the store owner replied. "He usually loves to look at himself in the mirror and talk."

"I don't have a mirror."

"Well, there's the problem. Buy a mirror, and he'll talk all night."

The man purchased a mirror, took it home, installed it in the cage, and waited. Nothing. He returned to the store.

"I can't believe it, sir. Why, when we had him here in the store, he would look in his mirror, ring his bell, and talk up a storm."

The man purchased the bell.

I'll spare you the rest of the joke, but as you can no doubt imagine, it goes on and on with more attachments being added until finally the bird drops dead. The reason was simple; the parrot had all the bells and whistles but no food!

There have been times in my life when I could relate to that.

Christian bookstores and the religious section of any major book chain are crammed with bells and whistles galore. There are books on every possible aspect of loving and serving God. Obviously I am not criticizing that; I am part of that system of communication. But I am asking why in the midst of so much information do we often remain spiritually starved? Why is there so little lasting change in our lives? If loving God is the most joyful, meaningful experience available to human beings, why do we seem to miss it?

Perhaps our everyday life takes all of our time and energy...but God waits patiently for our attention. He doesn't demand our loyalty and love, but he longs for it. Isn't it strange that although we are aware our real, eternal life is with God, we spend so little time investing in it? I don't mean this as a condemnation. I speak to my own heart and mind. Hearts can be easily moved, but minds take a while to change.

CHANGING OUR MINDS

I was twenty-five years old and working with British Youth for Christ in England. Every year we cosponsored with *Buzz* (a British evangelical magazine) an event titled Spring Harvest. Thousands of young people from Scotland, England, Ireland, and Wales would gather for a week of worship and teaching. I remember the first time that Argentinean evangelist Louis Palau was with us. His message was on the human will. He asked us what we thought it meant to take up our cross every day and follow Jesus. I knew that there was more to it than hacking up the kitchen table and dragging it through the street, but I wasn't clear what we are actually called to do. The evangelist described it this way: "Every time your will crosses the will of God, you drag your will in line with his."

That sounded simple, but lived out on a daily basis, it's very challenging, almost impossible—almost. The pull of our human nature, the desire to sin, is powerful. Habits are hard to break, as are lifetime patterns of wrong thinking. But as Andrew Murray said, "The Spirit teaches me to yield my will entirely to the will of the Father."

I have never been very overweight, but at five feet three inches, ten or fifteen pounds can make quite a difference. I was raised in a home and culture where sweets and desserts were seen as our God-given right. That's probably why you have never seen a Scottish Miss Universe! Barry does not have a sweet tooth; he is a chips-and-salsa man, so we don't keep a lot of candy or cookies in the house...unless my sister or mother are coming from Scotland to stay with us! Then the battle begins. Before they visit, I do self-talk for weeks.

Remember last time?

Remember how much you ate and how bad you felt and how none of your pants fit?

You don't need a whole bar of chocolate. You could have just one piece.

You don't have to eat a gallon of ice cream; a small bowl would be good.

Celery—good, brownies—bad.

As I greet my loved ones at the airport, I am bolstered by my firm determination and commitment. Even as they unpack and present enough candy to sink a dinghy, I smile kindly and place it all on a shelf not easily reached by human hands. For the first couple of days my halo remains intact. I serve dessert for everyone else and smugly polish my apple. By the third or forth evening, however, I have convinced myself that it would be good to join in with just a small bowl of ice cream, purely for the fellowship. By the end of the week I am down in the kitchen after everyone else has gone to bed, wolfing it down as if I were in a competition. I do it every time! It takes me about a month after they've returned home to be found clothed in my right mind and in my own jeans.

Why do I do it? I get so mad at myself, but it's a strongly rooted habit with enormous emotional baggage. I think, *If I eat this, I'll feel all cozy and homey.* But the truth is that I just feel fat and sleepy.

Habits are hard to break. Mark Twain said that they can't be thrown out the window; they have to be walked down the stairs one step at a time. It would be so much easier if we could just trash them, but that doesn't seem to work. We have to make a choice, a choice that we will make over and over and over again until the new pattern of behavior is as familiar as the old.

If that is true in physical matters, it is surely true in the spiritual realm. How do we drag our will in line with the will of God? How do we replace old behavior patterns with ones that draw us closer to his heart? I think one way is to dispel some of the wrong patterns of thinking that we have about God. See if you find yourself anywhere in this list.

If I surrender everything to God, then he'll take it from me.

God is out to get me, and if I make a mistake, he'll punish me.

The will of God is like a tightrope; if I make a wrong move, I'll fall off.

If I'd made different choices, God would have blessed me more.

If I give to God, he'll give to me—how I want, what I want, and when I want it.

If I can get rid of the unconfessed sin in my life, God will heal me.

If I totally surrender my will to God, he'll make me do something I hate.

I need to have everyone else's approval to be happy.

God expects me to meet the needs of everyone around me.

God only uses people who get it all right.

The list could go on and on, but when we view God this way, it's hard to drag our will in line with his. There is a difference between denying ourselves out of love for God and obeying out of fear of being annihilated by him. How sad it would be to spend our whole life on this earth caged by wrong beliefs.

Leo Tolstoy wrote a marvelous little book entitled *The Death of Ivan Ilyich*. It is considered one of the greatest pieces of literature written on the subject of death and dying. I admit that doesn't sound very cheery, but it has a profound lesson to teach. The subject of this short study is a successful middle-aged high court judge so absorbed with his own career that he has never given his mortality a second thought. When it becomes clear to Ivan that he is actually dying and that his active, brilliant mind is trapped in a body that is being ravaged by disease, he is horrified at how little time he has left. On his deathbed he looks up to see his son kissing his hand. He sees his wife with fresh tears on her face. He wants to tell them that he is sorry, but he doesn't have the strength to get the words out. He tries to say "forgive," but it comes out as "forget." So he decides that all he has left to give them is his death; he closes his eyes and dies with a world of unspoken words inside him.

Ilyich is the antithesis of Tolstoy, who, although he was a believer, was obsessed with a fear of death for most of his life. When one of his sons died as a very young child, Tolstoy ran from the house as if death were a virus he might catch if he stayed in the room with the boy's vacant body. Both Tolstoy and Ilyich were tormented by their belief systems. They lived lives that were irrevocably changed by the way they thought or refused to think about life and death.

I wonder how many of the people who fill church pews across our nation are silently tormented by their belief systems. I don't want to end my life with regret, wondering bitterly how I could have been so derailed by wrong thinking. There is a battle going on around and inside us. It's a battle for the mind. There is a battle with our culture, a battle with our brokenness, and a battle with the spiritual forces of darkness. So before we are able to love God with all our mind, we must address the damage in these arenas and in Jesus' name reclaim what is true and noble and good.

A BATTLE WITH POP CULTURE

A man was trying to decide which one of fraternal twin sisters he should marry. One girl was staggeringly beautiful but...intellectually challenged. Her voice was grating and harsh. Her laughter could peel paint off a wall, but she was extremely beautiful. The other sister was exceptionally plain, nay...ugly. Her eyebrows met in the middle like a reclining ferret, but she had the voice of an angel. When she sang, people wept. She was kind and wise but with the body hair of a yak. What a dilemma. Which one should he marry? He thought and thought and finally decided to marry the one with the voice of an angel. His family praised his wisdom. The couple was married with great ceremony, although people did comment on how dark it seemed inside the church. The next morning the groom woke up just as the sun was beginning to dance across his bride's pillow.

"Good morning, husband dear!" she said.

He looked at her for a moment and said, "Oh, for goodness' sake...sing something!"

We live in a culture where appearance is prized over character and honor. The pursuit of youth and lasting beauty is a multimillion-dollar business in our country alone. The latest craze seems to be Botox. This serum is a strain of botulism, a toxin that can grow in poorly pre-served food. Now you can have it injected directly into the muscles of your forehead or around your eyes so that you can't frown and cause wrinkles. Of course, you walk around looking surprised for about six months.

Scripture says clearly, "Charm is deceptive, and beauty is fleeting; but a woman who fears the LORD is to be praised" (Proverbs 31:30). As Christian women, how do we live in this world and not be squeezed into its mold? It's a battle I still struggle with. I have my hair colored every month, not to change the shade but to cover the gray. If I didn't have it done, I would end up looking like a skunk. I use face creams and eye creams, I shave my legs (a pursuit I intend to continue, having once roomed with a German nature-loving girl who could have plaited the hair on her legs). I use makeup and paint my nails. So am I con-forming to a pattern that is exposed in Proverbs as being a fleeting, triv-ial vanity?

I do these things because I like them and I like the way they make me look, but they don't tell me who I am. That's the danger we have to avoid. We are sold these products with the promise that they will change how we feel about ourselves and how others value us. Like the emperor's new clothes, we have been sold a promise as vapid as ice in the sun; it will not last. But I bought into those lies for a long, long time. I used to be tormented by my external appearance. People might look at me now as an attractive woman in her midforties, fairly slim (as long as the Scottish contingent has gone home), and well groomed. But I had a rough start.

The loss of my father when I was young was a devastating blow. His extreme personality change from a warm, kind dad to an angry, violent one left me with some very convincing and damning internal audiotapes. I felt ugly. As a teenager I had bad skin, and that was a huge torment to me. I hated to look at myself in a mirror. I bought all sorts of creams that were supposed to help, but they made little difference. I was a few sizes larger than I am now. More than all of that, my internal mirror was damaged. I got into financial trouble in my twenties because I bought clothes I couldn't afford, hoping that if I dressed the outside in something new, the inside might feel better. It never did. But my mind was stuck. It was stuck in the lie that if I could just change the way I looked, I would feel better.

Are you stuck there now? If you are, my heart aches for you. It is a miserable, lonely mind-set. When we carry such negative pictures of ourselves everywhere we go, it isolates us. I would try to diet around other people, but then I would end up sitting alone in the bathroom with a Snickers bar. Eventually my skin cleared up, and I lost some weight. I began working in television, so I had a wardrobe provided for me. What I found out then was that the things I thought would make me feel better didn't. When I looked in the mirror, the reflection told me I was thinner and more attractive, but inside I felt just the same. My depression began to take over in small, insidious ways. I began to withdraw from people. I began to eat less. I talked quietly. It was as if I were disappearing little by little. That's what I wanted to do. I didn't want to kill myself; I just didn't want to be here anymore.

Let's stop for a moment and think about the tapes that play in our heads. Do you believe that you would be more valuable and loved if you were thinner, taller, prettier, whiter, blacker, younger? We are drawn to those whose appearance is what our culture decides is the standard, the plumb line that we are held up to. In Turkey they love big women, the fatter the better. I have been so tempted to go to live there. I don't think the writer of Proverbs 31 was saying that beauty is to be despised, just that it is fleeting, so if you build your whole life on it, you will find in time that you have no firm place to stand. "Your beauty should not come from outward adornment," wrote the apostle Peter, "such as braided hair and the wearing of gold jewelry and fine clothes. Instead, it should be that of your inner self, the unfading beauty of a gentle and quiet spirit, which is of great worth in God's sight" (1 Peter 3:3-4).

Some women interpret this passage to mean that as long as they dress plainly, rejecting exterior adornments, they are pleasing God. That's not what the passage says. It says that our *beauty* should not come from those things. Our beauty should come from our internal rest in Christ—a quiet spirit, kindness, and gentleness. You can be externally plain and still be internally bitter and judgmental. The "inner self" is our character. It's who we are when no one else is watching us.

So the next time you hear those old tapes saying you are ugly, a failure, worthless, and less than others, remember that you are precious to God. He loves you and treasures you. Don't fall for the old lies. Replace them with eternal truth: "I praise you because I am fearfully and wonderfully made; your works are wonderful, I know that full well" (Psalm 139:14).

You might want to write that verse down and put it where you will see it every day. Retrain your mind to reject the foolish standards of our culture and embrace the Word of God.

THE BATTLE WITH OUR BROKENNESS

For some of us the battle for our mind is more than the damage done by the hype of television and magazines; it is an internal brokenness. If I had to sum up the first thirty-five years of my life in one phrase it would be this: *external success and internal desolation.* A shade too dramatic perhaps? It is obviously an overstatement. I have had many wonderful people in my life. I was raised by a godly, kind, and understanding mother. I have had many opportunities to see God use my life in ways that far exceeded anything I could have imagined. But there has always been an internal winter, a cold wind blowing through my soul, a familiar sadness. Perhaps you understand that. Those of us with a tendency toward depression experience it in different ways and express it with different words, but the underlying feelings of being disconnected, sad, and anchorless are the same.

Even though we are in a new millennium, there is still a shocking ignorance about the medical veracity of clinical depression. Many who struggle are encouraged to pray more, pull themselves together, or just snap out of it! But on this earth we deal with brokenness in many areas, one being the mind. When I began to slip, it was into a hole so deep and black that I never thought I would find my way out. I was right, but Jesus found me. My friend Bob Bennett wrote a song that perfectly describes how I felt. It's called "Man of the Tombs."

> Man of the tombs, he lives in a place where no one
> goes.
> He tears at himself and lives with a pain that no one
> knows.
> He counts himself dead among the living.
> He knows no mercy and no forgiving.
> Deep in the night he's driven to cry out loud.
> Can you hear him cry out loud?

Man of the tombs, possessed by an unseen enemy,
He breaks every chain but mistakes his freedom for
    being free.
Shame and shamelessness equally there,
Like a random toss of a coin in the air.
Man of the tombs, he's driven to cry out loud.

Underneath this thing that I've become
A fading memory of flesh and blood.
I curse the womb; I bless the grave.
I've lost my heart; I cannot be saved.
Like those who fear me, I'm afraid.
Like those I've hurt, I can feel pain.
Naked now, before my sin
These stones that cut against my skin.
Some try to touch me, but no one can.
Man of the tombs, I am.

Down at the shoreline two sets of footprints meet.
One voice is screaming; the other voice begins to speak.
In only a moment and only a word the evil departs like
    a thundering herd.
Man of the tombs, he hears this cry out loud.

Underneath this thing that you've become
I see a man of flesh and blood.
I give you life beyond the grave.
I heal your heart; I've come to save.
No need to fear; be not afraid.
This man of sorrows knows your pain.
I come to take away your sin
And bear its marks against my skin.

When no one can touch you, still I can,
For Son of God, I am.

Dressed now and seated clean in spirit and healthy of
    mind,
Man of the tombs, he begs to follow but must stay
    behind.
He'll return to his family with stories to tell
Of mercy and madness, of heaven and hell.
Man of the tombs, soon he will cry out loud.

Underneath this thing that I once was, I am a man of
    flesh and blood.
I have a life beyond the grave; I've found my heart; I
    can now be saved.
No need to fear, I am not afraid.
This man of sorrows knows my name.
He comes to take away our sin
And bear its marks upon his skin.
I'm telling you this story, because man of the tombs
    I was.

I love this song. I bless the day that Bob was inspired to write it and ache at the painful place in his life from which the ink must have flowed.

Some people experience a miracle, an instant gift from God. Once they were sick; now they are well. Once they were dying, and now they are vital. If that's your story, I celebrate with you. If, like me, your healing is a daily process dependent on the grace and mercy of God and the help of others, I gladly walk with you. Part of dealing with life on a broken planet is making peace with the fact that it is a broken planet. Nothing works as it was intended to. I still feel the pull of depression at times, but the desolation has been replaced by an absolute conviction that even if I walk through the valley of the shadow of death, even there—even there!—I will walk with Jesus…for nothing in heaven or hell can separate me from his love. Nothing! Nothing! Nothing!

You may battle with a different form of brokenness. Perhaps it's not a broken spirit but a broken body. There is a woman who comes to our conference in Houston, Texas, every year. I have only known her in a wheelchair. At times her multiple sclerosis seems to be in remission, but just as life slips into a pattern that seems bearable, the illness stretches its tentacles and grabs another part of her body, rendering it immobile.

When I saw her in the fall of 2002, I said, "You always seem so bright and peaceful. You smile, you extend grace to those who rush past you, bumping into your wheelchair unaware of how their needs might trample on yours. Is that hard for you, or are you just naturally that way?"

She laughed. "Are you kidding! Sometimes I want to scream, 'Get out of my way!' I have to choose every day, sometimes minute by minute, to set my mind on honoring God whether I want to or not. I have no physical strength to offer. The only strength I have is in my mind, my will. That's what I have to give."

Her words deeply affected me. I have physical strength that she doesn't have, but the internal battle she fights every day, the battle with the mind, is common territory. Like her, I am called to intentionally harness my will and my mind and bring them under the control and rule of Christ. I often fail, just as my wheelchair-bound friend confessed she does. But when I fail, I have a place to go.

> Praise the LORD, O my soul,
>   and forget not all his benefits—
> who forgives all your sins
>   and heals all your diseases,

who redeems your life from the pit
    and crowns you with love and compassion,
who satisfies your desires with good things
    so that your youth is renewed like the eagle's.
(Psalm 103:2-5)

THE BATTLE WITH SPIRITUAL DARKNESS

One of my favorite classes at seminary focused on the literature of C. S. Lewis. I had read some of his books before, but I enjoyed the forum of a small classroom setting that encouraged discussion. We looked at ten of his books. One of those was *The Screwtape Letters*. If you've never read this book, I would encourage you to get a copy. It's an interesting and engaging read and reminds us of the reality of an enemy set on our destruction.

The idea for the book came to Lewis one Sunday morning in church. It would be a series of letters written from a retired devil, Screwtape, to his nephew, Wormwood, a young recruit who has just been given his first assignment. Lewis wrote in an academic culture that smiled at his belief in devils as if his ideas were simply the material of Sunday school lessons on temptation. But as Lewis himself said, "There are two equal and opposite errors into which our race can fall about the devils. One is to disbelieve in their existence. The other is to believe, and to feel an excessive and unhealthy interest in them."

Lewis's intent in this small book was to make believers aware of the presence of an unseen spiritual realm that is at work around us every day with Satan and his host of fallen angels constantly trying to manipulate the hearts and minds of men and women. It's easy to forget what we can't see, but just as we serve a God who is passionate in his pursuit of us, we have an enemy who is hellishly passionate in his determination to cause as many of God's children to fall away as possible.

In some of Screwtape's letters to his nephew, we get a glimpse of life from the other side of the cross. Wormwood's first charge is a young man who has recently become a Christian—or gone over to the enemy's side as Screwtape sees it. Screwtape tells his nephew to discourage his charge from praying, to whisper to him that God doesn't answer prayer so why bother? He counsels the young devil to keep the man away from the Bible and other believers who might encourage and strengthen his faith and to attempt to lead him into sexual temptation, as that is an ideal way to make mortals fall.

The four areas that Screwtape focuses on are worth noting. He wants Christians to:

Stop praying.

Stop reading the Bible.

Stop fellowshipping with other believers.

Put themselves in the way of sexual temptation.

So let's flip that around, and we have a simple plan. Talk to God constantly. Pray for your family, pray for our nation and our president. Immerse yourself in the Word of God. Remember how Jesus combated Satan in the wilderness; it was with Scripture, not his own words. Surround yourself with godly people who love Jesus and want to live for him. Stay away from those who would pull you away from God and his people. I don't mean that we should avoid being salt and light in the world, befriending those who have no relationship with Jesus so we can introduce them to the missing piece of their lives. Far from it. That's our great commission. But don't neglect being with those who build you up in your faith. You'll never find a perfect church, so stop looking for it. Find a place and people you can throw yourself in with, those who love Jesus and try to live by his words. Don't put yourself in the way of sexual temptation. It may seem fun and harmless to flirt. You may long for more romance than you are experiencing in your life at the moment. But remember that behind the warm eyes and welcoming smile of someone who is not your spouse lies an enemy out to ruin as much of your life and family as he can.

I was heartbroken when I read in our newspaper here in Nashville of a pastor in a large church in our state, a good, godly man, who had stepped down because of an encounter he had with someone in his congregation. He had just written a book, a book I'm sure would have helped a lot of people, but his publisher has dropped the project because of his moral failure. How I ached for him. Do you really think that twenty or thirty minutes of sex with anyone is worth that? It always looks so good, so easy, and innocent at first, but it is one of Satan's primary weapons against us. He can't make us sin, but he can put it right in front of us.

So what do we do? Never, ever underestimate the importance of the discipline of putting on your spiritual armor.

> Finally, be strong in the Lord and in his mighty power.
> Put on the full armor of God so that you can take your
> stand against the devil's schemes. For our struggle is not
> against flesh and blood, but against the rulers, against the
> authorities, against the powers of this dark world and
> against the spiritual forces of evil in the heavenly realms.
> Therefore put on the full armor of God, so that when the
> day of evil comes, you may be able to stand your ground,
> and after you have done everything, to stand. Stand firm
> then, with the belt of truth buckled around your waist,
> with the breastplate of righteousness in place, and with
> your feet fitted with the readiness that comes from the
> gospel of peace. In addition to all this, take up the shield
> of faith, with which you can extinguish all the flaming
> arrows of the evil one. Take the helmet of salvation and
> the sword of the Spirit, which is the word of God. And
> pray in the Spirit on all occasions with all kinds of prayers
> and requests. With this in mind, be alert and always keep
> on praying for all the saints. (Ephesians 6:10-18)

At age five Christian knew what piece of armor went where and what it was for. I watched him one night go through a song he'd learned at school, and as he put on his helmet of salvation and his belt of truth, I suddenly realized that I don't do that anymore. I was watching my son and thinking how cute he is when the Holy Spirit reminded me that this is not "cute"; it's armor, and it has a purpose.

I find that the daily discipline of putting on my armor reminds me of every area in which I am vulnerable. I may feel foolish at first as I go through this symbolic exercise, but I'd rather feel a little foolish than walk out into this world unprotected. There is great strength in recognizing our weakness apart from God. When we bring all we are and have to him, he will protect our hearts and minds in this world and will give us peace. He has promised that to us. "Do not be anxious about anything, but in everything, by prayer and petition, with thanksgiving, present your requests to God. And the peace of God, which transcends all understanding, will guard your hearts and your minds in Christ Jesus" (Philippians 4:6-7).

We are called to love God with our whole heart and soul and with our mind, focused and determined. But what does it look like to love God with all our strength?

Now choose life, so that you and your children may live
and that you may love the LORD your God,
listen to his voice, and hold fast to him.
For the LORD is your life.

DEUTERONOMY 30:19-20

So do not throw away your confidence;
it will be richly rewarded.
You need to persevere so that
when you have done the will of God,
you will receive what he has promised.

HEBREWS 10:35-36

Create in me a pure heart, O God,
and renew a steadfast spirit within me.

PSALM 51:10

CHAPTER EIGHT

HEARTS ON FIRE

Loving God with All Our Strength

I remember the moment I met my husband. I was living in Southern California, attending Fuller Seminary. One evening when I got back to my apartment, there was a message on my answering machine from someone named Barry who was head of programming at the Trinity Broadcasting Network. He asked me if I wanted to be a guest on the *Praise the Lord* show. I did not. I had been involved with religious broadcasting for more than five years, and I decided I was entitled to at least one year off for good behavior! I returned his call and thanked him but told him I was going to pass. He was very polite and understanding.

A couple of weeks later he called again. He told me that friends of mine were going to be on the show in a couple of days and asked if I would like to be on with them. I have no idea why, but I said yes. I showed up at the studio about an hour before airtime. I didn't know what Barry looked like or how old he was, but as I walked through the door, I saw a man leaning against the wall who seemed to have stepped out of the pages of Greek mythology. It was Barry. We stood for a few moments staring at each other as if we were in a sappy movie scene. It was truly pathetic. Finally someone broke into our space and asked Barry if everyone had been in makeup. He asked me if I needed any makeup, and I asked him if there was a room with a mirror as I had forgotten what I looked like. He told me to follow him. He took me up to his office and sat at his desk gawking at me as I attempted to put lipstick on my lips and not my chin.

Finally it was airtime. I later discovered that it was Barry's birthday, and he had friends waiting to take him out for dinner, but he stayed in the studio to make sure everything went smoothly. Finally, after they told him they were leaving, he went with them. The next day I left for a two-week trip to Scotland. I bought several postcards to send to him to thank him for taking such good care of me on the show. I must have considered at least ten of them.

Too friendly!

Too remote!

You sound like his sister!

You sound like his mother!

Finally I settled on one and mailed it before I chickened out. When I got back home, I found a message from Barry on my machine, inviting me out for lunch. I called the Greek god back, and we turned the date into dinner. It seemed in those first weeks and months as if I were a woman with a fever. I was distracted from everything except when I would see him or what I would wear when I did. It was a delicious sickness.

I long for that kind of passion in my relationship with Christ. I want everything I do to be fueled by a love that engages every fiber of my being. I want to be so consumed by my love for God that everything else is framed by that. I believe that kind of relationship comes only from a fresh vision of Christ. There are several instances in the Old Testament that illustrate the impact of an encounter with the Lamb of God. It changes everything.

THE VISION

I turned around to see the voice that was speaking to
me. And when I turned I saw seven golden lampstands,
and among the lampstands was someone "like a son of
man," dressed in a robe reaching down to his feet and
with a golden sash around his chest. His head and hair

were white like wool, as white as snow, and his eyes
were like blazing fire. His feet were like bronze glowing
in a furnace, and his voice was like the sound of rushing waters. In his right hand he held seven stars, and
out of his mouth came a sharp double-edged sword.
His face was like the sun shining in all its brilliance.

When I saw him, I fell at his feet as though dead.
(Revelation 1:12-17)

"I fell at his feet as though dead!" That would seem an appropriate
response from the apostle John. What must it have been like to be
gifted with this vision of the Son of God—brilliant, fierce, and completely beyond any human experience?

The vision is recorded in the last book in the New Testament, the
Revelation of Jesus Christ. The Greek word used for *revelation* in this
context is *apokalypsis,* which means to expose in full view what was pre-
viously hidden, obscure, or secret. In the New Testament this word
occurs exclusively in the context of a divine disclosure. That is what the
book of the Revelation is all about. It gives us Christ's words to the
early churches and a behind-the-scenes look at all that is to come.

I confess that I find Revelation a hard book to study and understand. It is traditionally held that the author was the John who wrote
the fourth gospel. John at this point in his life was a pastor, but he
wrote as a poet. The visions he described are fantastic and spectacular.
At the beginning of his vision John was told to take a scroll and write
down what he saw and deliver it to the seven Asian churches—Ephesus,
Smyrna, Pergamum, Thyatira, Sardis, Philadelphia, and Laodicea. Each
church had a specific message addressed to them, and yet it's clear that
each church was to receive all seven messages. Two of the letters contain no words of judgment (Smyrna, Philadelphia), and two contain
no word of approval (Sardis, Laodicea). Since all seven letters would be
sent to each church, it would seem that Christ intended all the

churches to hear the words of both praise and error and learn from them. We can learn from them too.

It's the message to the church at Ephesus that's of particular interest as we consider what it means to love God with all our strength. Before Jesus spoke his words of reproach to them, he said: "I know your deeds, your hard work and your perseverance. I know that you cannot tolerate wicked men, that you have tested those who claim to be apostles but are not, and have found them false. You have persevered and have endured hardships for my name, and have not grown weary" (Revelation 2:2-3).

That's a pretty good résumé, wouldn't you agree? The Ephesians worked tirelessly for the sake of the gospel. They fought to maintain the integrity of the apostolic line. Life was hard for them as followers of Christ, yet they never complained.

But then comes the criticism: "Yet I hold this against you: You have forsaken your first love" (Revelation 2:4). They had served God faithfully and with perseverance, yet their hearts had fallen out of love with Christ. What had tainted that love, or had the flame simply died down over time?

Ephesus was known to be a corrupt city. It was the center for the worship of the fertility goddess known as Diana to the Romans and Artemis to the Greeks. The temple that housed the statue of Artemis in Ephesus was a spectacular place regarded as one of the wonders of the ancient world. Thousands of priests and priestesses were involved in the service of Artemis, many of whom were cult prostitutes. It was a debauched, depraved religion. One of Ephesus's own citizens, the philosopher Heraclitus, said that the inhabitants of the city "lived lives of terrible uncleanness."

The church at Ephesus was probably founded jointly by Aquila and Priscilla and later by the apostle Paul. So what pulled the church in this city away from her first love? Was it the spiritual climate of seduction and self-serving gratification that eroded Jesus' followers' love for Christ? I don't think so. Jesus said in his message to them that they worked very hard for the gospel, making no spiritual compromise. About fifteen years after John wrote Revelation, Ignatius, the bishop of Antioch, wrote to the church of Ephesus and commended them for refusing to welcome any heresy. So that was not the fault here. It was an issue of the heart.

The church had always been commended as a loving one. The Ephesians loved the Lord, and they loved one another. "For this reason, ever since I heard about your faith in the Lord Jesus and your love for all the saints, I have not stopped giving thanks for you, remembering you in my prayers," wrote Paul (Ephesians 1:15). It seems that when God made his pronouncement against the Ephesians, they were working as hard as always but without the initial passion that a young bride feels for her bridegroom. The Greek word used for *forsaken* in Revelation 2:4 is the word for "let go." These early believers were busy; no one could fault their activity for the sake of Christ. But their hearts were not on fire anymore. They had let go of their first love. They were as full of action as ever, but their service had become fueled by habit rather than passion.

I identify with that. It is so easy to be consumed by "Christian service" instead of being consumed by our love for Christ. That was Jesus' assertion when he visited his friends Mary and Martha. Luke 10 tells us that during Jesus' visit, Mary sat at his feet drinking in every word while Martha ran around anxiously getting everything ready for their guests. She was the perfect hostess, but Jesus says that there are more important things in life than rushing around getting everything ready, for then we might miss spending time enjoying the company of a loved one. Jesus knew that Martha loved him and wanted to serve him, but she had let her priorities get out of focus.

How many times at Thanksgiving or Christmas do you collapse at the end of the day under a mountain of dishes and the carcass of a ravaged turkey and realize that you haven't had time to talk with anyone? It can be the same with our relationship with God. Sunday, God's declared day of rest, has turned into one of the most stressful days for many families. Just getting the family ready for church and out of the door can be a mammoth undertaking. Life is too short and precious to allow it to be consumed by a to-do list.

FIRST THINGS FIRST

In our culture today we commend those who get a lot done and would probably view Mary's lack of action the way her sister did—as not particularly useful, perhaps even irresponsible. I admit I find "doing for" God and others easier than sitting at Christ's feet in rapt and adoring attention. But God longs for our hearts to be consumed with love for him and for our relationships with others to be fueled by the strength of that love.

I have a vivid image of my first Christmas with Barry after we married. I was looking forward to decorating our tree. We set off one evening for a store that specialized in Christmas decorations. I imagined that we would wander up and down, taking our time, lovingly gazing at each ornament and each other. I was still looking at the first wreath I had picked up, and I turned to ask Barry what he thought. I couldn't see him in my aisle. I assumed that he had moved on to aisle two. He was actually at the checkout with a full cart wondering what on earth I was doing. I was so mad that I sat down on the floor and refused to leave. (And you thought children were the only ones to pout!) Finally he sat down beside me and asked me why we were sitting on the floor in aisle fourteen.

"I want to do this together," I said.

"We are," he replied. "You found a wreath, and I got the rest."

Barry is a man with a plan. He gets up every day with a list of things to accomplish, and he gets to it. In stores he can make his way up and down aisles at Olympian speed. Over the years we have learned to meet each other around aisle seven. Seriously, though, we lose touch with each other because there is so much to do in any given day, and we find ourselves at bedtime wondering where the day went. I'm sure that's why there are so many sexual intimacy problems in marriage. True intimacy doesn't occur three minutes after you brush your teeth. "Making love can mean looking into each other's eyes," writes Catherine de Huech Doherty. "It can mean holding hands tightly. It means being aware of each other in the midst of a crowd. So it is with prayer. In the intense stillness of a loving heart all of a person strains toward the beloved."

One of the glorious things about our spiritual lives is that the closer we become to God, the more alive we are to all of life and the better relationships we have with everyone else. The more we love and worship God, inviting him into every room, the more we are able to experience true intimacy with those we love, not just in marriage but in all our significant relationships.

Stop for a moment and think about two or three of the most important people in your life. What do you know about them today that you didn't understand a year ago? How often do you talk, really talk, and not just pass on information? Do you know what their struggles are today, their hopes and fears? Most of us won't open up unless we know that time is being offered, and genuine care and companionship.

Most of us are overcommitted. My editor, Traci Mullins, and I have an ongoing joke of sorts that next year will be better, we won't be so overwhelmed, and we'll take on fewer projects. But it is a serious issue. So much of the disquiet that people experience internally is simply an accumulation of "stuff" that we never unload. We wander through our lives feeling disconnected from what's important. I realize my husband and I will not have a good marriage if we don't invest it with time we don't have and energy we can't spare. Other things can wait, but the eternal part of us—the part that is called to give our all in relationship with God and to love others as ourselves—can't wait.

Christ's warning to the church in Ephesus continued, "Remember the height from which you have fallen! Repent and do the things you did at first. If you do not repent, I will come to you and remove your lampstand from its place" (Revelation 2:5).

What does it mean for a church to lose its lampstand? What does that say to us today? There are many meanings suggested by different commentaries, but a significant one for us in this context is that our primary calling after loving God is to be a light to the world. Jesus said, "You are the light of the world. A city on a hill cannot be hidden. Neither do people light a lamp and put it under a bowl. Instead they put it on its stand, and it gives light to everyone in the house. In the same way, let your light shine before men, that they may see your good deeds and praise your Father in heaven" (Matthew 5:14-16).

Ancient towns were often built of white limestone, so they shone in the sun and could be seen for miles. At night the oil lamps that illuminated every home would shed their radiance over the surrounding area. The cities could not be hidden, and the analogy is clear: We are to let the "lights" of our own spiritual lives shine so brightly that no one could possibly miss the glow.

I never miss a prayer meeting! you may be thinking. But have you forsaken your first love?

I give more than I have to! But have you forsaken your first love?

I stick with my husband even though I'm miserable! But have you forsaken your first love?

I honor God even though he hasn't given me the desires of my heart! But have you forsaken your first love?

I serve God faithfully in spite of everything I've suffered! But have you forsaken your first love?

We can't sidestep the issue of loving God with all our passion and strength. God wants our hearts, not just our hands.

One of the gifts I received during my time in the psychiatric hospital was an understanding that I had based so much of my Christian life on doing rather than on being. I wanted to impress God with my tireless service even to the point of exhaustion. But when all of that fell apart and I wasn't able to do anything more than sit at his feet, I discovered what to me is home base. That's where God's children belong. Then everything we seek to do for God will overflow from an ardent love for him and a desire to worship him with our lives.

Do you feel close to God, or does he seem far away? Is it easier to perform an activity for him than to simply be in his presence? We need to stay in love. He wants nothing less.

So what happens to us on this journey? I want to look at our life with Christ as the writer to the Hebrews described it:

> Therefore, since we are surrounded by such a great
> cloud of witnesses, let us throw off everything that
> hinders and the sin that so easily entangles, and let us
> run with perseverance the race marked out for us. Let
> us fix our eyes on Jesus, the author and perfecter of our
> faith, who for the joy set before him endured the cross,
> scorning its shame, and sat down at the right hand of
> the throne of God. (Hebrews 12:1-2)

RUNNING

"Mom, when I grow up, will I be boring?" my son asked me one evening after dinner.

"Boring! You? Based on my experience of you from the day you were born until now, I would say no!" I replied. "Remember, you were the boy who made it snow at our home when it wasn't snowing anywhere else in Nashville."

He grinned at the memory. It was Christmas Eve, and Christian was seriously disappointed that there was no snow. "I wish it would snow too," I told him. "We don't always get snow in Nashville at this time of the year."

"I can make it snow!" he said.

"You can?" I asked, amazed once more at my son's conviction that he can do just about anything.

"Yes, I can," he replied. "Do you still have that big bag of flour that we opened to make cookies?"

"I do."

"Will you get it, Mom?" he asked.

I dragged this large sack of flour into the kitchen as Christian called for his dad to come and be part of our Christmas miracle. Christian explained how we were going to make it snow. Barry and I looked at each other, shrugged, and joined in. We all took large handfuls of flour and threw it up in the air, and it snowed in our kitchen that Christmas Eve.

Reminding him of the fun we had that night, I asked, "Why would you think you would be boring?"

"Well, I talked to a boy in preschool, and he said to me, 'You had better enjoy your life now, because I've looked at my parents, and they are bored!' "

Perhaps that's what has happened to many of us. Life didn't turn out quite as we expected, and as we muddle through our days, we realize that we have lost our zest along the way. Albert Einstein said, "The tragedy of life is what dies inside a man while he lives." Many of the people I talk with share their sense of futility in what they do on a daily basis. They have lost their spark for life and even for God.

In the spring of 2002, Barry, Christian, and I took a cruise through Alaska's Inland Passage. It was a magnificent trip. The scenery was breathtaking, and we loved seeing black bears and bald eagles in their natural habitat. We watched humpback whales perform their gracious water dance to an audience of clapping seals. The highlight of the trip for us was the day that we went dogsledding. We disembarked at one of the ports and were taken by bus to a helicopter pad a few miles away. Christian was ecstatic. We flew high up into the mountains of Skagway, over waterfalls and glaciers, and landed at the snow camp. Two hundred snow dogs stay at the camp for four or five months of the year.

Our guide asked Christian if he would like to be the lead musher on the dogsled.

"Yes ma'am!" he said with the confidence of a navy SEAL.

She showed him where to stand at the back of the sled, where his brakes were, and how to give the dogs voice commands. Then she passed on this piece of advice: "If you fall off, roll over and laugh a lot."

I loved that. It's become my new life motto! "If you fall off, roll over and laugh a lot." It applies in my relationship with Christ, but only when I trust God, love him, and believe he loves me. Love sets us free to do things we would never otherwise attempt. As we continue to look at all that really matters in our lives, it's clear that unless we have a strong foundation built on who God is and how much he loves us, we will always play it safe in life, feeling more like spectators in the race than participants.

You don't have to watch your life go by, standing on the sidelines of the race God has called you to run with strength and perseverance. You can run with power and confidence, knowing that it's all right if you fall, because you are loved, you are loved, you are loved!

Perhaps when you look at Mary and Martha, you think that Martha was the one who was using her strength to love Christ; she was a model of purposeful activity. Christ, however, commended Mary. The strength Mary showed was a different strength. It was a commitment to channel her energy into getting to know Christ more intimately so that her heart would be set on fire with love for him. Running the race is more than doing things. It's letting go of everything that clings to us and clinging instead to Christ.

Barry and I have made Wednesday our "date night." At first we tended to gravitate toward catching the latest movie, but we've begun to change the face of our time together. Sometimes we just go out for a leisurely dinner or take a drive out into the countryside for a picnic. We make room to talk, really talk. We have traded side-by-side community, which is good and has its place, for face-to-face companionship, which

both of us have come to realize we desperately want. Intimate relationships are essential for inner strength, for sometimes in the middle of our
race, an obstacle appears from nowhere, and we are left bloodied and
bruised on the track.

FALLING

We drove in silence, the flashing lights of the ambulance ahead almost
out of view.

"Give us a few minutes," the paramedic had said. "Let us get to the
hospital a little ahead of you."

I had nodded my head, numb and cold and sick at heart. I thought
of silly things. *I have his Christmas present. I guess I can take it back or
give it to someone else—Cliff, perhaps. He likes Cliff.*

Christian didn't say a word. I caught his reflection in the rearview
mirror as we passed under some bright streetlights. He was staring
straight ahead. His thumb was in his mouth, a morsel of reinforcement
for unfamiliar territory.

We sat in a small room at the hospital for a few moments. A nurse
brought Christian a Blue's Clues puzzle. I thanked her for her kindness,
wondering if she knew that Christian loved that show on Nickelodeon.
Of course not, I thought. *No one knows us here.*

"I'll wait with your son," she said. "The doctor would like to talk
to you."

I wanted to get down on the floor with the puzzle. I didn't want to
hear what I knew I would hear. I stood in front of the doctor and
looked into his eyes as he told me that William was dead. *You have
kind eyes,* I thought. *I wonder how often you do this and if you get used
to it.*

After I had spent some time saying good-bye to my father-in-law,
I went into the rest room and splashed cold water on my face. I col-
lected Christian, and we walked in silence to the car.

"Is Papa coming home tonight?" he asked.

"No, darling. Papa is not coming home tonight."

"I will miss him," he replied, understanding more than I realized. As we drove home, I saw tears like pebbles roll down his cheeks.

Weeks passed, months turned over, and I watched my son grieve. One evening as we walked together across a nearby golf course, he asked me why God took his Papa. I tried to explain in words that would mean something to a four-year-old boy.

"God didn't answer my prayer," he said.

"What prayer, sweet boy?"

"When we were driving to the hospital, I asked God to make Papa better, and he didn't do it. Why?"

Why? Why? Why?

So many books have been written on the subject of suffering, of unanswered questions, of knowing, as Jesus did, that sometimes when we get up off our knees in our own Garden of Gethsemane, God's answer is no. Perhaps that is what has extinguished the flame of your love for God.

I have never been able to find words to cover the wound in my son's soul. I weep with him; I stand with him in empathy holding two things to be absolutely true: God is good, and life is hard. He asked me one day if it will always hurt. I told him that I think it will, just not so bad.

My friend Nancy Guthrie has written a book called *Holding On to Hope: A Pathway Through Suffering to the Heart of God.* It chronicles the journey that she and her husband, David, and son, Matthew, took through the suffering and death of their child Hope because of a rare genetic disorder, Zellweger's syndrome. Zellweger babies don't live to see their first birthday. Hope had a little less than seven months.

David Van Biema, a writer for *Time* magazine, heard of the Guthries' story and approached them about interviewing them for an article. They agreed. David spent time with the family, asking questions and watching how they responded to difficult days. He visited the small Bible study group that Nancy and her husband and Barry and I are a part of and asked questions of those of us there that night. His questions probed the tender area of a belief in a good God and the reality of a dying child. David made it clear to Nancy that he didn't share their faith, but after the *Time* article came out, he wrote this for the cover of Nancy's book: "Few people have lived—and continue to live—as deep a firsthand experience of pain and loss. For that reason alone her Christian reading of the book of Job should lay special claim on readers themselves undergoing suffering. But there are other inducements: the clarity, grit, and honesty with which Guthrie explains how she has maintained hope and deepened faith where most would find only heartbreak."

Nancy quotes a passage from Hebrews in her book. "During the days of Jesus' life on earth, he offered up prayers and petitions with loud cries and tears to the one who could save him from death, and he was heard because of his reverent submission" (Hebrews 5:7). The writer says that *Jesus was heard*…but he still died. He was heard, but his prayer for rescue was not answered. When Nancy prayed for Hope, she didn't pray for healing. She prayed that God's will would be accomplished and that he would give her family strength when their own strength was gone. There are times in life when all you can do is gather up everything you know to be true and simply get back up and keep running. Often we are gifted with moments of grace, when Christ's presence seems very near, and at other moments we just keep running because God is worth it.

That reality is part of our lives on this planet. Falling is part of the race. There will be moments when our love for God will be tested in a furnace. Will we still love and serve him even when he doesn't do what we ask him to do?

Perhaps you are lying on the track right now, bloodied and bruised. I take great comfort in Christ's words as recorded in Matthew's gospel: "Are you tired? Worn out? Burned out on religion? Come to me. Get away with me and you'll recover your life. I'll show you how to take a real rest. Walk with me and work with me—watch how I do it. Learn the unforced rhythms of grace. I won't lay anything heavy or ill-fitting on you. Keep company with me and you'll learn to live freely and lightly" (Matthew 11:28-30, MSG).

What a wonderful promise: When we get alone with Jesus, we will recover our lives. Falling is very much a part of the race, but when we get back up, we run differently. We remember where we are going.

The call to love God with all our strength implies that the nature of our journey is long and often hard. Perhaps you have made it through a crisis, but rather than experiencing relief, you dread what else might lie ahead on the track. Will you make it to the finish line?

FINISHING

"I quit!"

I couldn't believe Christian's adamant defection from soccer camp. "You were doing great," I said.

"I still quit. It's too hot, and there's way too much running around."

I identify with the sentiment. Have you ever felt that way about something in your life?

That's it.

I quit!

This is just too much.

I've made it through some tough things with you, Lord, but this one is more than I can bear.

I was sitting at my desk on a spring morning, doodling on a pad of paper. *Shall I grow my hair longer or cut it shorter? Shall I keep the blond highlights or go for copper? Should I go back to my natural color, and do I still have a natural color?* Deep, spiritual issues! The phone rang. It was my doctor. I assumed he was calling to congratulate me on the good news that his nurse had passed on that morning. I have a family history of high cholesterol. My father had a heart attack in his thirties, so my doctor had agreed to my request for a Lifescan test. It's a test similar to an MRI. The test gives a clear picture of the heart chambers, arteries, and blood vessels from every angle. The nurse had called to say that everything was clear, no plaque and good blood flow. I was relieved. I didn't feel as if anything was wrong, but it's always good to know. My assumption about Dr. Leichner's call was wrong.

"I'm sorry to have to tell you this, Sheila, but they have discovered a lesion on your liver."

I sat in silence, staring at the suddenly ridiculous words on my notepad. "You will need to be at the hospital by 5:30 tomorrow morning for your scheduled CAT scan," the doctor explained. He prayed with me, and then he was gone.

I looked up, and Barry was standing at my office door. "Pat told me that Dr. Leichner called," he said. "Is everything okay?"

"No," I said. "They've found a lesion on my liver, and I have to go for a CAT scan tomorrow morning. I should be back in time to take Christian on his school trip. They're going to the Rainforest Café. I said I'd go. I said I'd drive. I should be back by then."

I rambled on and on and on. Barry put his hand on my shoulder.

"I'm sorry, but I need to be alone for a bit," I said. I went into the bathroom and sat on the cold marble floor. I tried not to think. I tried not to remember what it had been like to watch my mother-in-law die of liver cancer. I e-mailed a few of my best friends and asked them to pray for us. I just didn't want to talk to anyone in person. I couldn't sleep that night. I wandered around the house having an internal dialogue with God.

"What will I do if I'm sick?"

I'll be there.

"But what about Christian? He's so little."

I'll be there.

"I know that ultimately things are okay when we love and trust you, but sometimes they are not okay at the moment."

I'll be there. I'm here right now.

"Lord, help me. I'm afraid. I don't think I can do this. I don't want to do this. Does it always have to be so hard?"

I am here, and I love you.

"How did you do it, Lord? How did you face what was ahead? You knew that the outcome would cost you everything. How did you do it? Why did you do it?"

I love you. I love you. I love you.

Finally at four in the morning, I took a shower and sat outside. It was still dark and so quiet. I thought about calling my mom, since it was ten in the morning in Scotland, but I decided against it. There would be time enough for that after I knew one way or the other. I drove to the hospital, the same place I had driven to in the dark following William's ambulance. I checked in, signed all the paperwork, and gave them my insurance card. As I waited, I wondered about those who don't have insurance. Do they get tested, or do they just wait to see if an internal terrorist is taking over their body?

A nurse called me back to a room and gave me a glass of liquid to drink. "Drink all of this," she said.

"What does it taste like?" I asked.

"It's horrible."

"What if I bring it back up?" I said.

"Don't."

I swallowed it down trying not to gag. In about thirty minutes I was taken for the CAT scan.

"I feel as if I've got a little fire inside me," I told the technician.

"That's normal," she said. "You'll feel as if you need to go to the bathroom, but you won't.'

You hope I won't, I thought.

I lay on a bed that moved into a tunnel. The technician talked to me through a speaker and told me when I had to hold my breath and for how long. I left the hospital at half past seven and drove home. Christian was up.

"Hi, Mom. Today's the big day! We're going to the Rainforest Café! We're going to the Rainforest Café!"

Barry offered to go in my place, but I welcomed the diversion. When you're in charge of four four-year-old boys, it's hard to think about anything else. I watched Christian stick his hand in the mouth of a large plastic hippopotamus and pretend that it was tearing him limb from limb. All the other boys laughed. I wanted this to be his world, a world of bikes and friends, of school and church, of kitchen snowstorms and flushing the latest two fish.

Later at home Barry and I waited. That's all we could do—wait. The phone rang. I didn't answer it. My secretary asked me if I would come up to her office. I climbed the stairs, sick to my stomach, and took the receiver from her. Barry stood by the window.

"I got the results back," Dr. Leichner said. "I pushed them to rush it as I knew how you would be feeling. You're all clear, Sheila! It was a birthmark that showed up on the scan. You've had it all your life."

I thanked him and hung up. I told Barry and Pat, and they burst into tears. I didn't feel the relief that I expected. I was grateful, but the good news seemed as unreal as the bad news had. I was on an emotional roller coaster, and I wasn't sure where the next drop was.

That's the hard thing about finishing this race we're in. We don't know what is around the corner. Perhaps we have fallen farther down the track and have managed to get back up again, but what's around the corner? That's when we need to return to the twelfth chapter of Hebrews: "Keep your eyes on Jesus, who both began and finished this race we're in. Study how he did it" (12:1, MSG). Jesus did it by total obedience to God the Father. His love for God blazed through every day of his life. We read of how he would often pull away from the crowd, even his closest friends, to be alone with his Father. We don't know what took place in these meetings, but Christ obviously drew strength from being in the presence of God. Jesus wasn't following rules in his pursuit of his Father; he was living out the passion of his being.

KEEPING LOVE ALIVE

Barry and I were married in Charleston, South Carolina. We spent a week there a few months before the wedding, making plans and booking the florist, the caterer, the hall, and the band. Looking back now, I'm not sure why we bothered. Nothing turned out as we expected. The caterer let us look at several sample menus. We wanted to have a buffet, but we wanted it to be an elegant affair. My detail-oriented husband-to-be took over and worked hard to ensure smooth sailing on the big day.

The whole event was a comedy of errors. Barry's dad booked the funeral limousine, as it was cheaper than the wedding one. When I finally learned that fact, it helped explain the solemn demeanor of the driver and the respectful hush of pedestrians as we drove to the church. William's bow tie was missing when the tuxedo was delivered, which whipped Barry's mom into a frenzy until she collapsed in a chair in the bride's room and informed me, "I am a zombie!" After the service the second car left all the bridesmaids at the church, and the driver who was supposed to take Barry and me got drunk and left!

But the food was the highpoint. Barry and I arrived at the hall for the reception, and the great, sumptuous banquet that we had ordered looked like a small picnic for a raccoon. I assumed they were just bringing the food out, but the caterer explained that perhaps he had underestimated a little, and that was all he had. He informed me that they had made a special food basket for Barry and me to take back to our hotel after the reception. "I think you'll be pleased," he said, ignoring our starving guests. When it was time for us to leave, Barry went to get the basket from the kitchen and was informed that they were very sorry but someone had set fire to it! We laughed all the way to the hotel. (Barry's dad drove us.)

It's a terrible thing to run out of food or beverages at a wedding. "When the wine was gone, Jesus' mother said to him, 'They have no more wine'" (John 2:3). In her book *Just Give Me Jesus,* Anne Graham Lotz reviews what happened at the wedding in Cana. She writes, "I doubt there was any major catastrophe like the waiter dropping a dozen bottles of wine in the kitchen. I expect the wine ran out one glass at a time until it was gone."

That's how it seems to be with our love for God. The passion of our first love doesn't disappear overnight. It takes weeks and months, even years of neglect, of letting go of everything that keeps love alive. We don't wake up one morning and decide not to talk to God anymore. Rather we squeeze him out of our lives with business, family commitments, work, ambition, money, or simply a failure to make our relationship with God our top priority. Remember what A. W. Tozer said: "What comes to mind when we think about God is the most important thing about us."

As I have studied in preparation for writing this book, God has set fire to my heart all over again. As I read how Jesus lived, what he did for love of you and me, I am overwhelmed by this kind of love. We romantics fantasize about the perfect mate who will ride into the disorder or boredom of our lives and, by his presence, change everything. He is here. His name is Jesus. He is worth everything we can bring. He is worth loving with all our heart, soul, mind, and strength.

Jesus has left us a simple plan—to love God and our neighbor. It's all that really matters in this world. It's a plan that will transform our lives and in doing so transform the lives of those around us. But who is our neighbor? Does loving like that mean we have to let others walk all over us? Let's take a look.

If I speak in the tongues of men and of angels, but have not love,
I am only a resounding gong or a clanging cymbal.

1 CORINTHIANS 13:1

To return evil for good is the devil's way:
to return good for good is man's:
to return good for evil is God's.

ARCHIBALD HUNTER

You have heard that it was said,
"Love your neighbor and hate your enemy."
But I tell you: Love your enemies
and pray for those who persecute you.

MATTHEW 5:43-44

CHAPTER NINE

NO MORE PASSING BY

Loving with a Heart Like God's

I was watching the evening news, moved by the plea of a father on behalf of his child. "Please pray that my daughter will be returned safely to her family." The camera zoomed in and captured the anguish in his eyes, a man pleading to a nation not to forget his daughter, Heather Mercer, or her friend Dayna Curry.

I was familiar with the story. Two young American girls had been imprisoned in Afghanistan for proselytizing, sharing their Christianity with those of another faith—in this case, Muslim men and women. Their situation seemed bleak. They had been taken prisoner on August 3, weeks before the tragedy of September 11, 2001, but now as the dust began to settle on the decimated site where the World Trade Center had once stood, we were at war with the Taliban, the oppressive rulers who had forced their will on the Afghan people. The Taliban was protecting Osama bin Laden and his al-Qaeda forces, and believing them to be responsible for the bombing, U.S. forces had begun nightly bombing raids on suspected hideouts. Ground troops were combing the mountainous terrain seeking to oust the terrorists. Somewhere in that country the two girls were being held prisoner. They faced danger on all sides. It was a very real possibility that they would be executed by the religious police who had arrested them or even killed by an American bomb dropped on the town where they were being held.

As the news interview came to an end, Heather's and Dayna's photos appeared on the television screen. They looked to be in their early twenties—sweet, smiling girls in happier times. I began to pray, along with thousands of others around the globe, that God would protect them and return them safely home. When the news was released several weeks later that they had been liberated, I cried with joy. On their return to America they were interviewed by Larry King, appeared on the network news channels, and were able to talk a little about how God had protected them. I wanted to hear the whole story, so I was delighted when I heard that they were to be our guest speakers at a few Women of Faith conferences in 2002.

They are lovely young women, full of joy and passion for Jesus Christ and committed to the spiritual freedom of the Afghan people. They spoke just before I did on Friday night. Dayna spoke first. She talked about her years of seeking God in college and the pain of an abortion. Then she met a group of young people who were passionately in love with Jesus. As she gave herself to Christ, she offered up her whole life to go wherever God would send her. God sent her to Afghanistan.

She told us of the spiritual hunger there and yet how difficult it was to spend time with the Afghan women. The religious police were vigilant in their commitment to keep Western women away from Muslim women. If a Muslim woman was seen talking to someone from the West, she would be severely beaten or imprisoned.

Dayna then told us about the day she was arrested and the terror of that experience as she was pushed into a vehicle by men with guns and whips. "But it was God's plan for good!" she said, her face shining under the stage lights. "The police had tried to keep us away from the Afghan women, and then they threw us into prison with them. Praise God!" Even as the audience laughed with her and shared her joy, I thought, *Only God could do that.* Only God can so wash human eyes that in a place of darkness and fear they saw his light and grace.

Dayna went on to tell us of the nights of prayer and singing, times of fear and doubt, and then their ultimate liberation when the Northern Alliance drove the Taliban troops out of the town where they were being held. They made it through town and out into an abandoned airfield where, they had been told, American helicopters would pick them up. They waited, watching and listening for the choppers. Finally they heard them circling overhead, but it was dark, and the pilot couldn't see them.

Finally Heather took a head covering that had been a treasured gift, poured a little oil from their lamp on it, and set it on fire. They added everything they had—their blankets, pieces of wood, anything they could find. The pilot saw the flames, and the young women were finally picked up. I cried as I listened to Dayna tell of the joy of that moment. One of the soldiers told her, "I want you to know that since the first day of your captivity on August 3, my family and I have never stopped praying for you." Dayna and Heather had been in prison for 105 days.

Heather spoke passionately about their love for the women and children of Afghanistan. "We were told not to go. We were told that these people did not want to know about Jesus. That was a lie. They are hungry to hear the name of Jesus and to be prayed for in that name." She told us of their work with orphans, with the unloved and unheard.

A mother asked them to come to a local hospital and pray for her daughter in Jesus' name. The hospital was a nightmare of unsanitary conditions, dirty needles, lack of beds and clean sheets, if they had sheets at all. Heather made her way to the little girl's bed. She laid her hands on the child's head and prayed in the name of Jesus that he would touch her life. When Heather opened her eyes and turned to leave, there was a line of patients waiting for her to pray for them in the name of Jesus. They had never heard his name before. Can you imagine such a thing, never to have heard the name of Jesus? There can be no greater love for our neighbors than to introduce them to the love of their lives.

We think that if people have actually heard the name of Jesus, then they have been given an opportunity to grasp the reality of his love. That is far from the truth. I remember an encounter with a makeup artist on a photo shoot for a book cover. After a couple of hours she told me that she recognized me from my television shows on the Christian Broadcasting Network. "It must be nice to be in the club," she said.

"What do you mean?" I asked. "Do you mean those who are members of *The 700 Club*?"

"No, I mean God's club, the club for the holy ones, the ones who haven't messed up," she replied, a painful irony in her voice.

"God doesn't have a club for those who haven't messed up. He only has a place for those who have," I said.

She looked at me for a moment as if I had just told a drowning woman how to grasp on to a life buoy. "The whole point about our relationship with God," I explained, "is that we have all messed up, and that's why Jesus came, to pull us all out of the waves."

Every time I work with this woman now, our whole conversation is about the love of God. It's as if she is learning a whole new language. Tragically, there is a language of hate and judgment often associated with the Christian church, but we have the joy of translating the truth to our neighbors whether they work in our office or scrape to survive in a nation like Afghanistan.

The love of Jesus shone in Heather Mercer's eyes as she spoke to our audience, and the arena was filled with the sweet aroma of the presence of Christ. "I'm not very gifted," she had said to the Lord before she went to Afghanistan. "Can you use me?" Jesus simply asked her if she could love the poor and serve them in his name and weep with him for the lost. Her answer was a resounding yes!

KNIFE-EDGE MOMENTS

"Love your neighbor as yourself." This command appears eight times in the New Testament, echoing the command given centuries before to the children of Israel. Jesus is quoted delivering this text three times in Matthew's gospel alone, once in a teaching to his disciples, once in response to the rich young man who wanted to know what he had to do to inherit eternal life, and once to a Pharisee who was attempting to trap Christ in a sea of words. In Mark's gospel we have the account of the teacher we referred to in chapter 1 who genuinely wanted to find a way of wading through a sea of laws to find the most important one. The reference in Luke's gospel, however, the one we refer to as the story of the Good Samaritan, came from a completely different encounter. It still has much to teach us today.

Let's look at the passage and put Christ's response in context. A lawyer, in an attempt to entrap Jesus, asks him what he has to do to inherit eternal life. Jesus asks the lawyer what the Law says. "How do you read it?" Jesus asks (Luke 10:26). He can read this man's heart and carefully exposes him, giving him a chance to repent or be trapped by his own duplicity.

The lawyer readily quotes a passage from Leviticus: "'Love the Lord your God with all your heart and with all your soul and with all your strength and with all your mind'; and, 'Love your neighbor as yourself.'" Jesus tells him he's quite right, so now the lawyer is in trouble. It's obvious to the crowd that he just asked Jesus a question he already knew the answer to.

Here is one of those knife-edge moments. We are all given them. A moment of truth where we get to choose the path ahead. An encounter with God disguised in human flesh. Knife-edge moments define our character. They are gifts not to be taken lightly.

How the lawyer responds here will affect the rest of his life. Will he have the courage to accept the repercussions of his own pretense, or will he do all he can to save face? Missing the point of a critical encounter here, he opts to save face. "But he wanted to justify himself, so he asked Jesus, 'And who is my neighbor?'" (Luke 10:29).

In his book *Desiring God*, John Piper puts the lawyer's question another way: "Teacher, whom do I not have to love?" In essence that's what the lawyer is asking. "If I have to love my neighbor, be a little more specific. You can't mean...them. And I'm sure you're not suggesting...him...or that group of people over there."

Jesus doesn't even dignify the lawyer's question with an answer;

instead he tells a story. A man, probably a Jew, was traveling from Jerusalem to Jericho when he was attacked by robbers, beaten up, and left for dead on the side of the road. A priest and a Levite, God's temple agents, passed by without so much as a "Can I help?" Then a Samaritan entered the story, a man who by his ethnic background would be a pariah to the lawyer. But he was the one who stopped and helped. He did more than that. He behaved like God.

Jesus turns back to the flushed-faced lawyer and asks which man in the story behaved like a neighbor. The lawyer is furious, humiliated, shown up as a fool and a cheap trickster. He spits out his answer, that he supposes it would be the one who stopped and showed mercy. (Notice that he can't even bring himself to say the word *Samaritan*.) "That's right," Jesus said. "Now you go and live like that!"

The lawyer totally missed the point of God's command to love our neighbor. The command is not to prepare a guestlist of those worthy of receiving our love. It's the opposite of that. It's about having a heart like God's, quickly moved by compassion to help whoever is in need. There should be no hierarchy in the kingdom of God. Our neighbor is the one in front of us. Our neighbor is the one who stumbles on the side of the road. Our neighbor is the one bleeding on the inside. God commands us to extend love to whoever crosses our path. No more passing by. The other side of the road has been closed.

EMPOWERED BY THE SPIRIT

The apostle John tells us that it is not possible to love God with everything in us and not love our neighbor. "Anyone who claims to be in the light but hates his brother is still in the darkness. Whoever loves his brother lives in the light, and there is nothing in him to make him stumble" (1 John 2:9-10). So if we find ourselves with hatred and bitterness in our hearts—and who can pass through this world without picking up those rocks from time to time?—then we don't love God with everything we have. Perhaps we love him with our mind, an intellectual assent to the fact that he is definitely God, but our hearts are cold. Or conceivably we love him with our hearts, but we devote little of our mental energy to intentionally loving him. The second part of that same truth is that it is not always possible to love our neighbor without the love of God. We can't do it in our own strength.

Christian came home from school one day with a disturbed look on his face. He told me that one of the kids in his class had said she hated him.

"I don't know why she would say that, Mom."

"What did you say to her?" I asked.

"I just walked away. It made me sad."

I told Christian that if she said it again, he could tell her that he didn't hate her, because God asks us to love everyone. I saw hurt and indignation in my son's eyes. It's hard to love our neighbor when our neighbor doesn't want to be loved.

Our neighbor can be our spouse, our children, those we work and worship with. At times it is easier to show the love of God to a stranger than to someone in our own circle. One of my friends experienced that harsh reality. When she married her husband, he was a wealthy man from an affluent family. Her new mother-in-law was disgusted with her son's choice of a wife and with her Christian faith. She considered my friend beneath the social standing of her family and made life very unpleasant for her.

A few years after her son's marriage, the mother discovered that she had cancer. By this point her son wanted little or nothing to do with her. The only one left in the last days of her life was my friend. She cooked for her, bathed her, read to her, and kept a vigil by her bedside so that this bitter woman would not be alone. A few days before her mother-in-law died, my friend asked, "What about God?" The woman who had once been so hostile answered, "He must be here because you are." My friend had the joy of leading her mother-in-law to a relationship with Christ.

Loving our neighbor can seem like a thankless task, but it is a command of Christ. When we line up our will with the will of God, as my friend did, we experience a peace in knowing that no matter how our love is received, we are living our lives as Jesus asked us to.

DANGEROUS NEIGHBORS

Perhaps you're thinking, *Sheila, you don't know what you're asking. Surely Jesus doesn't expect me to love people who are set on hurting or destroying me!*

Jesus does indeed long for us to love as he loved, but I think many people misunderstand what that looks like in the face of abuse and evil.

"They tell me that I need to go back," she said, sobs racking her fragile body. "If I go back, he'll kill me, but they say that's in God's hands and I need to love as Jesus loved."

As I held this devastated, beaten-down woman, I thought once more how I wished that Jesus had commanded us to punch Pharisees in the face! I've looked and looked, and it's not there. We have used Scripture to torture one another, to twist it round someone's wrists as if we have taken them hostage spiritually. Jesus never told us to do that. Think of how he responded to evil. He *confronted* it, and then he *walked away.*

> Then Jesus asked them, "Which is lawful on the Sabbath: to do good or to do evil, to save life or to kill?" (Mark 3:4)

> Everyone who does evil hates the light, and will not come into the light for fear that his deeds will be exposed. (John 3:20)

When he had finished speaking, Jesus left and hid
himself from them. (John 12:36)

If we examine the battered woman in context of Jesus' command,
what does he say to her? "Love your neighbor as you love yourself." Is
that how she would treat herself? Would she walk around her house
banging her head against the wall? Would she break her own arm? Of
course not; that's ridiculous. To say to a woman who is genuinely afraid
for her life that she has to return to her abuser is spiritual cruelty. There
may be exceptions—times when someone has received special grace
from God to walk carefully and wisely with an abusive partner, but I
do not believe that God wants to use his Word to break our spirits and
have us live in fear.

One of the most popular Christian books in recent years is *Boundaries* by Henry Cloud and John Townsend. It teaches biblical principles
for relationships, focusing especially on how to live in difficult relationships in a way that honors God and our own lives. One of the lessons I learned through that book was how to raise an appropriate
boundary in a friendship that is becoming unhealthy. I had a friend
who believed that it was my responsibility to meet every need in her
life. If I wasn't able to do that, she became angry and verbally abusive.
She told me that God had shown her that. "You'll be Jesus to me!" she
announced one day as if I had applied for the job.

I asked her to meet me for lunch. "We have been friends for some
time, and I care about you," I said.

"You mean everything in the world to me too," she replied.

"That's not what I said. I care for you, but I am not Jesus, and I'm
not willing to carry messages back and forth from you to him. He loves
you. He wants to talk with you."

"You're just trying to get rid of me," she said.

"That's not true, but here's what is true. It's no longer all right for
you to yell at me and expect me to be at your beck and call day and

night. I want a friendship with you, but until your expectations change, don't call me. Think and pray about this for a couple of days, and then let's meet again and talk."

I never heard from her again.

We can be consumed if we feel that we have to meet the needs of everyone in our lives. We were not designed for that. Only God can meet all of our needs. Loving our neighbor is about respect and honor, kindness and eyes that are open to see. Mother Teresa will be remembered as one who saw Jesus in the eyes of the poor and dying of Calcutta, India, every day. But she loved people one at a time, one at a time. She said, "The whole work is only a drop in the ocean. But if we don't put the drop in, the ocean would be one drop less. Same thing for you. Same thing in your family. Same thing in the church where you go."

BEING JESUS TO ONE ANOTHER

Our world is full of lonely people, people who feel disconnected and unloved. In 2002 the television Emmy Awards made a special presentation to Oprah Winfrey for what was described as her humanitarian efforts. In her acceptance speech she said that after years of being in the public eye and thousands of television shows, the one constant cry of the human heart is that we want to matter. We want to know that we make a difference somewhere to someone. I have no idea where Oprah stands in relationship to Christ, but her description of the cry of our culture rings true.

As a society we have accumulated more stuff for the outside of our lives and less fabric for our internal tapestry. Jesus' command to love our neighbor is clearly the recipe to cure this interior malady. In Chuck Colson's wonderful book *Loving God,* he tells a story that illustrates this principle. Jack Swigert, the man who had piloted the *Apollo 13* mission to the moon, was hospitalized, his body devastated by cancer. A tall man sat by his side in the place he had been almost every evening since

Jack was admitted to the oncology ward. It was Bill Armstrong, the U.S. senator from Colorado. At that time, with the many roles he played in the Senate, he was one of the busiest men in Congress. But he sat by his friend's side and read Scripture to him.

Jack's breathing became labored. Senator Armstrong began to read Psalm 150: "Praise the LORD. Praise God in his sanctuary; praise him in his mighty heavens. Praise him for his acts of power; praise him for his surpassing greatness…"

Jack had stopped breathing. He was home free.

Who among us would not want to be handed into the arms of Jesus like that? That's loving your neighbor as yourself, doing for someone else what you would love someone to do for you, and because you love God, you do it whether it is reciprocated or not.

There is a character in Tolstoy's story about the high court judge, *The Death of Ivan Ilyich,* who behaves like Jesus to the ungrateful, bitter, dying Ilyich. His name is Gerasim, the pantry boy on Ilyich's household staff. He is a peasant—a simple, plain boy who always smiles no matter what he is asked to do. In the last days of his master's life, he is asked to perform all sorts of difficult chores. He is the one to help Ivan out of bed and onto a chamber pot to relieve himself. The judge has no strength left, so Gerasim pulls up his pants for him. When Gerasim gets him back into bed, Gerasim stands and holds Ilyich's legs up, as it makes the pain less. Tolstoy writes a simple line that says so much. Gerasim has been standing for some time holding up his master's legs, "And strangely enough, he thought he felt better while Gerasim was holding his legs."

Human touch is powerful; simple care is life changing. We all long to be held, to know that someone is truly present with us. I remember that when my mother-in-law, Eleanor, was dying of liver cancer, it was the little things that seemed to bring her some relief: massaging her feet, combing her hair, holding her hand, kissing her head. We are to be Jesus to one another in simple and powerful ways.

Christian's nanny, Sean, has been with us for two years. She travels with us so that, when I am at conference arenas, he has a buddy to take him to the zoo or the museum. Sean is an elementary schoolteacher but intends to pursue further education in medicine. In the fall of 2002 she signed up to volunteer at our local children's hospital to rock the babies in the intensive care unit. Many of the parents can't be there twenty-four hours a day, so the hospital has set up a system to ensure that these struggling little ones have the gift of human touch as much as possible.

There are thousands of ways to love our neighbor in Jesus' name. Tom Davies is a reporter for the prestigious British newspaper the *Observer*. In a lovely book, *Merlin the Magician and the Pacific Coast Highway*, he describes an encounter with a man and his dog on a beach. The man was throwing sticks into the water, and his delighted dog was fetching them. Not wanting to interrupt their time together, Tom prayed for them where he stood. "I sent him the love and security of a coming Christ. I surrounded him with my prayer, twirled it round his arms, body and neck. He picked up on it immediately and, surprised by sudden warmth, turned around and waved at me, smiling joyously."

In an often cold and lonely world we have been given the privilege of loving as Jesus loved, being his hands and feet and heart even as he teaches us how to love. There is a glorious paradox peculiar to our faith—in loving God, in loving others, we discover that we are loving ourselves as well. Our culture would encourage us to focus our attention on our own needs until we are consumed by them. The church too often tells us to find redemption by cloaking painful realities in an ill-fitting martyrdom. What does Jesus say about what it means to love ourselves?

Jesus loves me! this I know,

For the Bible tells me so;

Little ones to Him belong,

They are weak but He is strong.

ANNA B. WARNER

For God so loved the world

that he gave his one and only Son,

that whoever believes in him

shall not perish but have eternal life.

JOHN 3:16

God has given you a beautiful self.

There God dwells and loves you with the first love,

which precedes all human love.

You carry your own beautiful, deeply loved self

in your heart.

HENRI NOUWEN

CHAPTER TEN

I LOVE ME, I LOVE ME NOT

Seeing Ourselves As God Sees Us

My son came home from school one day during his first two weeks of kindergarten and informed his father and me that he had learned a dumb song that day.

"Why was it dumb?" I asked.

"Well, it says that God comes first, then everybody else, then me!"

"What's dumb about that?" I questioned.

"How can I put everybody before me? I'll never get to me!"

I understood his concern, but I've learned that the greatest joy in life is obeying the Word of God—even when it goes against everything inside us. The apostle Paul wrote to the early Christians in Galatia, "You, my brothers, were called to be free. But do not use your freedom to indulge the sinful nature; rather, serve one another in love. The entire law is summed up in a single command: 'Love your neighbor as yourself.' If you keep on biting and devouring each other, watch out or you will be destroyed by each other. So I say, live by the Spirit, and you will not gratify the desires of the sinful nature" (Galatians 5:13-16).

In a day when most of the ills of the world are chalked up to low self-esteem, this is a very significant passage. If the lawyer who tried to outwit Jesus in Luke 10 stumbled over the idea of "love your neighbor," we stumble over "as yourself." We read that part as if it *was* the command. We skip through the verse to those words and assume that the only way we can love our neighbor is if we get the loving ourselves bit down first. I've said it myself time after time, "How can I love my neighbor if I don't love myself?" But that's not how this passage reads. Jesus took the fact that we love ourselves as a given.

It seems he is saying that we are called to take care of others the way we already take care of ourselves. We feed ourselves, clothe ourselves, and care for ourselves in numerous ways, so we are to care for others in those ways too. "Love your neighbor" is the command, not "love yourself."

In *Desiring God,* John Piper writes, "Jesus is saying to the lawyer: Take note how much you love yourself, how you try to get the best place in the synagogues, how you seek to be seen praying in the streets, how you exercise all rigor to maintain purity. My command to you is this: Take all that zeal, that ingenuity, all that perseverance and with it seek your neighbor's well-being."

Today we can watch any talk show, scan the rows of self-help books, and hear the message to our culture loud and clear: "You are a wonderful human being who has been misunderstood and overlooked. If we can build up your self-esteem, all will be well with your world." If we abuse our children, it's because we have low self-esteem. If our marriages fail, it's because we didn't take care of ourselves well enough. As we guzzle our way through a mountain of fried food to a sea of blocked arteries, the excuse is that we don't feel good about ourselves. We are very concerned with "me."

I have the problem.

I have the potential.

I need to take care of me.

Now that our son is about to turn six, I see that our job for the next few years is to train him to think and live out his Christianity in the world. At his school the three "posts" that behavior are suspended from are respect, honor, and honesty. The students are taught that all human beings are precious because they are made in the image of God, but more than that, the children are encouraged to always put others before themselves. That is so contrary to our culture, where we are encouraged to take care of number one. That is *not* a biblical principle. We are exhorted to have the same mind as Christ had when he left behind all that was his to become all that is us. Paul writes, "Your attitude should be the same as that of Christ Jesus: Who, being in very nature God, did not consider equality with God something to be grasped, but made himself nothing, taking the very nature of a servant, being made in human likeness" (Philippians 2:5-7).

Remember my conversation with Christian in chapter 5 about his first exposure to Paul's words in Romans 3:23: "For all have sinned and fall short of the glory of God"?

"Does that mean I am a sinner?" he asked incredulously.

"Yes, Christian. You are a sinner."

Christian was horrified by the idea that his mom considered him a sinner. He is an only child, a cherished child given to a woman later in life, so it is a daily struggle to balance my input into his heart, mind, and ego. I want him to know he is loved, believed in, cared for, supported, and treasured, but the fact remains that Christian is a sinner as surely as I am and his father is. I don't have to teach him to love himself; it's there. I have to teach him to love God, to honor and respect others, to think more highly of them than he does of himself; those leanings are not naturally there.

As I have mentioned, I am a huge fan of the works of C. S. Lewis. I have read almost everything he has written. One of his sermons, "The Weight of Glory," clearly illustrates how we have turned virtue on its head. He writes that if you were to ask twenty men today what they considered to be the highest virtue, nineteen of them would say "unselfishness." He asserts that if we were to go back several hundred years and ask the saints of old, they would say "love."

"You see what has happened?" Lewis asks. "A negative term has been substituted for a positive and this is of more than philosophical importance. The negative ideal of Unselfishness carries with it the suggestion not primarily of securing good things for others, but of going without them ourselves, as if our abstinence and not their happiness was the important point."

Do you see the difference? Unselfishness is about me. Love is about you. If I love you as I love myself, I will lavish my life on you. I won't have to remind myself to be unselfish, because I'll be thinking about you anyway, loving you, wanting the best for you. On the other hand, when my focus is on being unselfish, I am absorbed with thoughts of myself: "How am I doing? What should I be giving up?" When love meets opposition, it still loves. When unselfishness meets opposition, it can so easily turn to self-righteousness or bitterness: "No one appreciates me!"

So too in our relationship with God. Do you love to worship, or do you find yourself looking at your watch thinking, "If they sing that chorus one more time, I'm out of here!" Worship can be a duty, or it can be a joyful overflow of love.

I remember when my husband got his new car. I was not allowed to drive it until he had it properly broken in (at least a year!). Anytime we went anywhere, I considered taking a sack lunch, as Barry would park what seemed like miles from where we were actually going so the car wouldn't get scratched. He polished it, patted it, and was appalled when Christian spilled a little cranberry juice on the floor mat. Barry had waited for the right car, and he loved it; he told his friends about it and smiled upon it like a gracious benefactor.

I'm exaggerating just a bit to communicate the point that worship should flow out of love, out of recognition that God is good and he is for us. We worship things all the time, things we value and have benefited from. Loving our neighbor as we love ourselves also should flow out of bounty. The ability to love as Jesus loved doesn't start with loving ourselves; it springs from our acknowledgment that God loves us beyond measure and that his love is so plenteous it has to spill out everywhere.

THE TWO FACES OF PRIDE

Our society seems to be divided into two distinct groups: those with an overinflated picture of who they are and those whose balloon burst so long ago they couldn't find it if you offered them a thousand dollars.

Pride is a strange bird. There is a pride that says, "I am worth it all. I am a wonderful human being, and if you don't see that, who needs you." There is a pride that says, "I'm not worth loving. How could God love me? I don't belong." Both separate us from the love of God. Both are a tainted reflection of what loving self looks like. In *The Cost of Discipleship* Dietrich Bonhoeffer wrote, "The life of discipleship can only be maintained as long as nothing is allowed to come between Christ and ourselves—neither the law, nor personal piety." So how do we arrive at a proper estimation of ourselves?

God's Word tells us clearly that we are wonderful and cherished creations. When God walked in human flesh, covered with the dust of the road and the tears of the people, he was saying with every step, "Look at me. This is what God is like."

God is not remote; he is here.

God is not cruel; he is kind.

God is not weak; he is strong.

God is not indifferent to your pain; he weeps with you.

God does not keep a record of wrongs; he washes you clean in a river of forgiveness.

God does not hate you; God loves you.

"Look at me," Jesus says to you and to me. "Do you see the cross, the rusted, tearing nails, the roar of anguish as darkness wraps me in all the foul, evil stench of who you are so that you can be where I am? This is the price I paid, willingly, for you. Do you see the price tag? Do you understand the value? Do not tell me you are not worth loving. I descended into hell because you are."

Scripture also tells us that God knows exactly what is taking place in our hearts: "For the word of God is living and active. Sharper than any double-edged sword, it penetrates even to dividing soul and spirit, joints and marrow; it judges the thoughts and attitudes of the heart. Nothing in all creation is hidden from God's sight. Everything is uncovered and laid bare before the eyes of him to whom we must give account" (Hebrews 4:12-13).

In my life it has been very important for me to know and accept the truth about myself. One of the most liberating verses I know is found in John's gospel: "Then you will know the truth, and the truth will set you free" (John 8:32). I used to read that as saying that when we know Jesus, who is the Truth, we are free from the condemnation of sin. But I think much more is there. I think that as we face all that is true about ourselves and bring it into the light of God's presence, we can be set free from the hold our sinful nature has on us when we keep it in the dark.

Pastor and author Steve Brown, quoting a friend, observed: "All of biblical theology can be summed up in two sentences:

"1. Cheer up, you're a lot worse than you think you are.

"2. Cheer up, God's grace is a lot bigger than you think it is."

I love that! Even in our "moments of truth," we have no idea how desperately evil our hearts can be. We have no concept of what perfection is, especially in the way in which God is perfect. We think if we manage to control our tongues, we are doing well, but thoughts can roam across our minds, consuming those who have no idea they are being stalked. If we don't drink or smoke, we pat ourselves on the back, but how often does our gluttony open a floodgate of undisciplined behavior? If we remain sexually pure, we thank God that we are not like others, even as in our minds we live a quite different life.

The truth is that we are lost without God. That doesn't stop being true when we commit our lives to Christ. We are daily lost without him. Anytime we are tempted to say, "Thank God I'm not like that!"

others observe something in us that causes them to say, "Thank God I'm not like that!"

But cheer up! God's grace is so much greater than we can ever imagine. For those of us who are afraid to stretch our wings in case we fall or fail, I would remind you of something we should carry with us every day. On the darkest day that earth will ever know, the perfect Lamb of God was butchered on a hill, nailed down so that we could rise up, pinned to the earth so that we could fly, his feet crushed and broken so that we could dance. Steve Brown says that too many of us are looking at our feet when we dance. "Dancing that requires that we look at our feet all the time is not dancing…it's marching. And, frankly too many people are marching. Jesus didn't come to make us good; he came to make us his."

Steve's wisdom is simple and splendid. When our focus is on ourselves, on being "good enough," we only make ourselves and those around us miserable.

Such a man was Leo Tolstoy. His life was a constant update of the long list of rules he imposed upon himself. He had rules for developing the will, rules for developing lofty feelings and eliminating base ones. He kept making his life smaller and smaller. He attempted to give away everything he owned. He wanted to free himself of his house, his clothes, and the rights to his books, all in a quest to be good enough for God. Several times during his marriage he took a vow of sexual abstinence, but as Philip Yancey points out in his book *The Jesus I Never Knew*, "He could never keep the vow for long and much to his shame Sonja's sixteen pregnancies broadcast to the world that inability."

One of the saddest things about self-righteousness is that it offers no warmth to others. Tolstoy's wife said of him, "There is so little genuine warmth about him; his kindness does not come from his heart but merely from his principles." She noted that history would honor him as a great writer and humanitarian but his children would not remember him that way. Rather, they would remember him as a man who never gave them as much as a cup of water. How sad! And how lonely Tolstoy's cage must have been to live in. It is clear from his letters and diaries that he was always an unhappy man. He kept as many of his rules as he could, but none of his efforts produced any warmth or peace for him or his loved ones.

Imagine how different it could have been. He was a wealthy man. He could have enjoyed that and taken great delight in sharing that wealth. He was a brilliant man, and his wife and children could have been bathed in the riches of that knowledge and been drawn closer to God. It's interesting that he freed all his servants, yet he lived in bondage himself. Many in his day were critical of his way of life. In personal letters he begged them not to judge God because of his inability to live up to God's laws: "If I know the way home and am walking along it drunkenly, is it any less the way because I am staggering from side to side?" The answer is no, but he seems to have been the only one who didn't believe it.

Do you feel bogged down in your desperation to get it all right? Are you constantly beating yourself up because you blew it again? Pride is not just something that rears its head when we think we have achieved a modicum of righteousness; it is equally present when we think we have failed yet again. Madeleine L'Engle described the burden this way in her poem entitled "Ascension, 1969."

> Pride is heavy.
> It weighs.
> It is a fatness of spirit,
> An overindulgence in self.
> This gluttony is earthbound
> Cannot be lifted up.
> Help me to fast,
> To lose this weight!

Otherwise, O Light One,
How can I rejoice in your
Ascension?

For those of us who think that we have so much to offer God, Martin Luther said: "What is it about our arrogance that makes us think that anything that we could do would ever be more adequate than the blood of God's own son?" For those of us who think that we are too bad to be loved, remember that Jesus did not come for those who have all their ducks in a row. "Jesus said, 'It is not the healthy who need a doctor, but the sick. But go and learn what this means: "I desire mercy, not sacrifice." For I have not come to call the righteous, but sinners'" (Matthew 9:12-13).

My son has an unusual style of whistling. Instead of blowing air out, he sucks it in. There is a whistling game that we love to play when we are traveling. Each of us whistles the melody of a song, and the other two have to guess what it is. The last time we played I was having a hard time guessing Christian's selection. He was getting positively red in the face sucking breath in. I thought he was going to pass out. Finally he gave in and yelled at me, "Mom, I'm going to die over here if you don't get it! It's 'Jesus Loves Me'!"

Don't die out there for lack of the love of God that he longs to pour from his open wounds into your broken heart. He wants nothing more than to set you free to love and be loved.

A FIRM FOUNDATION

"Love the Lord your God with all your heart and with all your soul and with all your strength and with all your mind"; and, "Love your neighbor as yourself."
(Luke 10:27)

There is nothing more important for us to give our hearts and minds to than this. Embracing these commands will revolutionize our lives if, by the power of the Holy Spirit, we commit ourselves to living them out in every arena.

I love to read. I am a passionate advocate of reading good books, but books won't change our lives. I am firmly committed to the ministry of Women of Faith. I have seen how God has blessed the lives of more than a million and a half women, but conferences won't change our lives. Only God by his Holy Spirit can transform us. But it's a joint venture. We work together with him, wholeheartedly pursuing him and carrying out his greatest commandments with all our strength. How we wish God would just fix us in the night while we are asleep so that we could wake up righteous. That's not going to happen. But we will fulfill our destiny if we determine to walk in Jesus' steps for the rest of our days—learning, falling, getting back up again, repenting, and worshiping—for he is life, and there is no life without him! Our lives, our families, our churches would be places of true joy and peace if this became our number-one pursuit.

When I talk of joy, I'm not referring to happiness but something much deeper. I received an e-mail from a college student who had read my book *Honestly,* which chronicles my journey with clinical depression. She, too, struggles with this and wrote one question: "Are you happy now?" I understood her question, but I'm not sure that my answer was what she was looking for. I told her that I have found a peace in my life and a joy that sings inside me on good days and bad days. The paradox is that joy is exposed in all its depth in the presence of sorrow, and happiness is exposed in all its frailty in the presence of sorrow. Walter Wangerin Jr.'s words are powerful in their truth: "The difference between shallow happiness and a deep sustaining joy is sorrow. Happiness lives where sorrow is not. When sorrow arrives, happiness dies. It can't stand pain. Joy, on the other hand, rises from sorrow and therefore can withstand all grief."

Joy is rooted in hope in God, which will never disappoint. Happiness is rooted in the circumstances of the day and is frequently fleeting. Often relationships suffer because we are not "happy." I enjoy great happiness in my life and relationships, but my commitment to love God and others cannot be rooted in whether or not I feel happy at the moment. You can study the Word of God cover to cover in as many translations as you like, and nowhere will you find that the aim of our lives is the pursuit of happiness. The Declaration of Independence of our great nation allows us to pursue it, but the Word of God commands us to pursue God and love him with everything we have.

We can make our walk with God about...

Reading our Bible
Going to church
Attending prayer meetings
Listening to Christian music
Reading Christian books and magazines
Attending conferences, etc., etc.

But what happens when the weather gets rough? What happens if your husband leaves you or your child dies or you discover you have breast cancer or you feel emotionally destitute? We have emphasized countless things in our Christian culture. Many are good and true, but it's like building a house with no firm foundation. When the weather gets rough, the house is coming down. It's the same in our spiritual life. The previous list will fail us every time if the foundation is not a passionate pursuit of God himself and a selfless love of the "neighbors" who live in our homes, our churches, and our workplaces. God's Word gives us plumb lines, not to self-righteously measure our spiritual progress, but to humble us and show us our need of him. Only his love can transform our human hearts.

The subtitle of this book is "Jesus' Simple Plan for a Transformed Life," but we are not transformed by following a new code or a better set of rules. We are transformed by loving God. John Piper suggests changing a preposition in a line from the famous Westminster Catechism: "The chief end of man is to glorify God and enjoy him forever." He proposes that we say instead, "The chief end of man is to glorify God by enjoying him forever." It's a small change but a huge one. The former implies that sometimes we'll glorify him, sometimes we'll enjoy him. The latter states clearly that the way to glorify God, to love and honor him, is to enjoy him.

Do you want to love yourself? Love God. Do you want to love your neighbor? Love God. Do you want to find your life? Love God.

Do yourself the biggest favor of your life. Love God.

> And we, who with unveiled faces all reflect the Lord's
> glory, are being transformed into his likeness with ever-
> increasing glory, which comes from the Lord, who is
> the Spirit. (2 Corinthians 3:18)

Listen, I tell you a mystery:
We will not all sleep, but we will all be changed—
in a flash, in the twinkling of an eye, at the last trumpet.
For the trumpet will sound,
the dead will be raised imperishable,
and we will be changed.

1 CORINTHIANS 15:51-52

Our Father's love is deeper and wider
than we typically imagine.
Like a buoy thrown to a drowning person,
grace must be embraced, recognized for what it is—
a gift that compels us into life
with gratitude and love.

DUDLEY J. DELFFS

Seek God's house in happy throng;
Crowded let his table be;
Mingle praises, prayer and song,
Singing to the Trinity.
Henceforth let your souls always
Make each morn an Easter Day.

GERARD MANLEY HOPKINS

Chapter Eleven

TRANSFORMED BY A LOVING GOD

Marveling at His Grace and Mercy

One night when I had finished reading Christian's Bible story to him, he decided that we should act it out. It was Jonah and the whale.

"All right, Mom, I'll be God, and you can be Jonah." I was relieved.

"I'll be God until you get on the boat, then I'll have to be the sailors," he continued with all the seriousness of a New York casting agent.

Everything went as expected until we got on the boat and the storm began to threaten the lives of the sailors.

"It's my fault!" I cried remorsefully. "I disobeyed God. If you throw me overboard, the storm will stop."

"No way, Mom! There's no way I'm throwing you overboard. We'll go down together!" (So much for the lost souls in Nineveh.)

What a sweet sentiment from a little boy. What an unspeakable gift from God.

I will not throw you overboard.
I will not let you drown.
I will not let you disappear.
I love you, and we are in this together.

Isn't that what we all want? Don't we all long to know that God is alive and speaking to us, that he knows where we are, what's going on, and what's about to happen? It's the deep longing of every heart. W. G. H. Holmes of India wrote of seeing Hindu worshipers tapping on trees, stones, and bushes and whispering, "Are you there? Are you there?"

We want to know we matter.

We want to know we are loved.

As amazing as it may sound, God not only loves us, he also longs for our company. God, the Almighty, longs to sit and eat supper with you and with me! That's what it says in Revelation 3:20: "Here I am! I stand at the door and knock. If anyone hears my voice and opens the door, I will come in and eat with him, and he with me." The Greek word used here for *eat* is the word used for the main evening meal. Not a snack or a quick lunch but the meal that you take time to enjoy, relishing one another's company.

So often we associate being in relationship with God with negative images.

Self-denial

Giving in

Taking up our cross

Resignation

Servile slavery

How sad! I think the whole purpose of our lives is to get the biggest holy kick to be found on this earth out of our relationship with God. I think if we really got to know God, we would wonder why we had waited so long. The glorious God of the universe—the one who threw the stars in place as if he were throwing confetti at a lavish wedding; the one who with a word parted the enormous wall of water that was the Red Sea to give his children a path to freedom; the one who took his very heart, wrapped it in bone and tissue, and placed it in a teenage girl to be spilled out onto hay on a dark night—longs to know and be known by us. Despite the fact that we have defied him since the day holy breath filled mortal lungs, God loves us. He cannot stop. He loves us. This God, the only God, longs for our company every moment.

The first word our son ever said was "Da Da." I will never forget the look on Barry's face. It was a priceless moment. I remember how I felt when Christian would look at me and smile, reach for my finger, and hold on tight. It was a joy so deep I thought my heart would break. Can you imagine how God our Father feels when we, his beloved children, look to him, reach for him, smile at him, and call his name? We need eyes to see him so that we will have hearts to respond to him with trust and devotion. We are invited to dine with the King on a daily basis, but so often we settle for a packed lunch as we head out the door with our own agenda.

In *Celebrating the Wrath of God,* Jim McGuiggan recounts a story he heard on good authority about a conversation that took place between a daddy camel and his son.

Son: "Dad, these two big humps on our backs, what are they for?"

Dad: "Well, there's not a lot of food in the vast deserts we travel in, so we're able to store up a lot of food in these humps of ours."

The conversation goes on and on with the small camel wanting to know what purpose each unusual feature of his anatomy serves. After the father has given detailed descriptions of how their bodies enable them to survive in the hot desert sand for weeks on end, the son has only one remaining question: "With all this equipment, what are we doing in the San Diego Zoo?"

Good question. With all we have and all we are as children of God, what are we doing where we are?

Sören Kierkegaard, the Danish writer and philosopher, loved to tell stories and parables to make his readers think. He told one about two men traveling by night. The wealthy man traveled in his well-lit carriage with his own lantern inside. He was safe and secure, insulated from the dark. As he provided his own light, there was no darkness around him. The poor peasant traveled with no lantern, just the light of the stars. His view was vast and glorious. He had no light of his own, so he was guided through the dark by God's spectacular display on the starry, starry night.

The meaning is clear. We can provide our own light, our own ideas, our own protection, or we can depend on God, on Christ, the Light of the World, to guide us through the dark night of life on this earth.

9/11

It was more than anyone could take in. I stood with the rest of the nation, the rest of the world, and watched what we had so easily taken for granted the previous day crumble like a sandcastle before our eyes. At first I thought I was watching a movie. Then my secretary came into the kitchen, her usual rosy complexion as gray as the dust that rained on the crowds as they ran from the fallout of the collapsing World Trade Center.

There are days in human history, usually marked with blood, that bring us close to the breaking point because they are beyond reason— so far beyond reason that they threaten us all with their madness. Days like the slaughter of innocents in Bethlehem, when the blood of baby boys mingled with the screams of tormented mothers. The worst day of all was that Friday on the hill of death, when the sky turned suffocating black at noon, and heaven and hell roared, one in agony and one in mistaken victory.

September 11, 2001, was a day of human agony and despair that God could feel as deeply as he did the nails in his hands. It was a day when thousands of people would be left, like Tolstoy's dying judge, Ivan Ilyich, with a world of words inside of them. Perhaps a man thinking of leaving his wife, torn in two directions, was pondering what to do as he entered his office building that early autumn morning. Perhaps a woman decided to keep the good news about her pregnancy to herself until that evening when there would be time to talk and rejoice. No one could have imagined what that day would bring.

Lisa and Todd Beamer were such people. They had a good marriage. Like most of us, they were working on it, but they had a plan for the future and a commitment to each other. They had two children and another one on the way. The issue that they were currently struggling to resolve was time. Todd had to travel so much with his job that he and Lisa felt the boys weren't getting as much of their dad's time as they needed. Ironically, it was Todd's recent commitment to spend more time with his boys that put him on that doomed flight on the morning of September 11. He could have traveled the day before from his business in one city to his business in the next, but instead he headed home to be with Lisa, David, and Drew between appointments.

Todd Beamer is internationally known now for his courageous phrase, "Let's roll," as he and the other passengers aboard United Airlines Flight 93 tried to reclaim the plane from the terrorists who had hijacked it. The plane, carrying forty passengers and crew, went down in a remote area southeast of Pittsburgh, Pennsylvania, killing everyone on board, yet saving possibly hundreds of others who were the target.

The first time I met Lisa was at a Women of Faith conference where she had been invited to speak. She was pregnant with Morgan, the little girl Todd would never meet on this earth. I was struck by Lisa's grace and composure, her quiet spirit, and her moving account of the transforming love of God that will hold us when we cannot hold ourselves. It had only been a few weeks since her husband's death, and yet I had seen her appear on all the major network news shows. I remember thinking how hard it must be to handle your pain in front of a watching world. Lisa is a very private person, and yet she allowed God to shine his light and comfort on a grieving nation through the hole in her heart and family.

A year later she was with us again at a conference in Philadelphia. She and I compared notes on how hard it is to let your first child go off to kindergarten. Christian had just started, and her son David would begin next summer. Again I was struck by the peace that rests upon her. Mary Graham, the president of Women of Faith, interviewed her and asked about her day-to-day life now that the first anniversary of September 11 had passed. She used the life of two-year-old Drew to answer.

"When Drew and I are walking across a parking lot, sometimes he doesn't want to go where I'm going, and he'll scream and pitch a fit. Sometimes he wants to slip his little hand out of mine and run ahead. But when he walks beside me, it works perfectly. When he does his own thing, it doesn't work so well. That's how it is in my relationship with God. Sometimes I want to pitch a fit or run ahead, but it's best when we walk hand in hand." It was such a simple but profound illustration of a life of trust and peace.

Lisa told us how God had prepared her for that awful September day many years before. As a teenager she lost her father, and the anguish she felt raised a barrier between her and God. For years she struggled to reconcile a loving God and her tragic loss until a passage in Romans shone through the fog of her despair and gave her light.

> Oh, the depth of the riches of the wisdom and
> knowledge of God!
> How unsearchable his judgments,
> and his paths beyond tracing out!
> "Who has known the mind of the Lord?
> Or who has been his counselor?"
> "Who has ever given to God,
> that God should repay him?"
> For from him and through him and to him are all things.
> To him be the glory forever! Amen.
> (Romans 11:33-36)

That passage became a gift to her, a bridge that walked her safely back to God. She was given a picture of the majesty and sovereignty of God that she could say yes to, despite her loss.

Just before September 11 she had been reading the passage again and remembered how God had poured his oil of healing on her grief. When she received the news that Todd was indeed on the plane that went down in Pennsylvania, she thanked God for reminding her of a time in the past where he had met her in the depths of her despair and been her very life and breath. When Todd's car was returned to her from the airport parking lot a few days after the tragedy, she asked friends if they would clean it out for her. They found a small stack of Scripture verses that Todd had beside him. The one on top said this:

> Oh, the depth of the riches of the wisdom and
> knowledge of God!
> How unsearchable his judgments,
> and his paths beyond tracing out!
> "Who has known the mind of the Lord?
> Or who has been his counselor?"
> "Who has ever given to God,
> that God should repay him?"
> For from him and through him and to him are all
> things.
> To him be the glory forever! Amen.

What a gift! It was a great comfort to Lisa to think that those words were in Todd's heart and mind that day.

Lisa says she continues to be transformed by a loving God—not overnight, not in the space of a year, but day by day as she learns to trust him step by step.

ON THIS ROCK

I have great empathy for Peter, the fisherman, follower of Christ. He was a passionate man, one who spoke his mind. He was a leader. He was also a follower.

> As Jesus was walking beside the Sea of Galilee, he saw
> two brothers, Simon called Peter and his brother
> Andrew. They were casting a net into the lake, for they
> were fishermen. "Come, follow me," Jesus said, "and I
> will make you fishers of men." At once they left their
> nets and followed him. (Matthew 4:18-20)

I find that scene remarkable. When we say that we are followers of Christ, we mean that we follow his teaching, the leading of the Holy Spirit. Peter and Andrew, however, literally dropped what they were doing and followed this man Jesus around for three years! They had no idea who he was at first. Even after all they saw, they still got it wrong, but they made Christ their lives.

One night some of the disciples were in a boat, and the water became so rough that they feared for their lives. Sometime between three and six o'clock in the morning, they saw a figure moving on the surface of the water. They were terrified, convinced that they were seeing a ghost or some otherworldly apparition. Jesus told them not to be afraid, that he was the one walking on water.

"'Lord, if it's you,' Peter replied, 'tell me to come to you on the water'" (Matthew 14:28). Jesus told him to come. I'm amazed that Peter took a single step out onto the rough sea. Most of the time when I hear this story told, the emphasis is on Peter's lack of faith as he became spooked and began to sink into the water, but I commend him for getting out of the boat at all! His heart was in the right place. He wanted to be with Jesus. He wanted to believe.

When Jesus moved on to Caesarea Philippi, a region abounding in pagan worship, he asked his disciples what the locals were saying about him.

> They replied, "Some say John the Baptist; others say
> Elijah; and still others, Jeremiah or one of the prophets."

"But what about you?" he asked. "Who do you say
I am?"

Simon Peter answered, "You are the Christ, the Son
of the living God." (Matthew 16:14-16)

In response to this declaration of faith, Jesus blessed Peter and gave
him the greatest commission of the church: "And I tell you that you are
Peter, and on this rock I will build my church, and the gates of Hades
will not overcome it" (Matthew 16:18).

Peter, James, and John had no idea that they were about to see
something that would shake them to the core. Jesus led them up to a
mountaintop. "There he was transfigured before them. His face shone
like the sun, and his clothes became as white as the light. Just then
there appeared before them Moses and Elijah, talking with Jesus"
(Matthew 17:2-3). Moses and Elijah had both beheld something of the
glory of God, but the light that shone that day was the light of Christ
himself, a glimpse of all that was and is to come. What must Peter have
thought when he lay down to sleep that night? Did he think that the
glory he saw on the mountain meant that Jesus the Messiah was going
to declare his kingdom now? The tide was soon to turn.

"I'll never leave you!" Peter had declared to Jesus. "I am ready to go
with you to prison and to death" (Luke 22:33). But night came, and as
he woke up in the garden with the sound of an angry mob in his ears,
he realized that he had fallen asleep again when Jesus had asked him to
stay awake with him in his dark hour. What was happening? Who were
these people? What was Judas doing?

Then Jesus was arrested and taken away, but where? Peter followed
at a distance. He didn't run away; he followed right into the courtyard
of the high priest. He had to come. He had told Jesus he'd always be
there for him, and then he'd fallen asleep. He sat by the fire in the
courtyard, trying to get the chill out of his bones.

A servant girl scrutinized him in the firelight. "This man was with him," she declared. "But he denied it. 'Woman, I don't know him,' he said" (Luke 22:57). If only he could get rid of her with that. But a little later, someone else recognized him as one of Jesus' followers. "No! I'm not one of them!" Peter replied. Still later, another asserted he most certainly was. "Man, I don't know what you're talking about!" Peter insisted (Luke 22:60).

The part of Peter's heart that brought him to this fire, that longed to be as brave as his rhetoric, was quickly overwhelmed by the human side that didn't want to be caught up in a rabble hungry for blood. Even as his last denial was spilling out of his mouth, the rooster crowed. Jesus looked Peter straight in the eye, and Peter recalled with horror the Lord's prediction earlier that day: "Before the rooster crows today, you will disown me three times" (Luke 22:61). Peter ran outside the courtyard and wept as men seldom do.

Where did he go that night? Did he go home, or did he wander the streets? Did he go back to the garden and pray?

The next day came and went. Peter was nowhere in sight. Where was he when the sky turned black as sin? Did he see this as God's judgment on him?

Sunday morning. The women had gone to care for Christ's body. Peter couldn't bring himself to go. He couldn't look at Jesus now. Life was over. Suddenly he and the other ten disciples heard noises, loud noises, excited voices. The women were back and were shouting all at once. They told the eleven men that the tomb was empty; angels had told them that Christ had risen from the dead! They were specifically instructed to tell the disciples *and Peter* that the resurrection had occurred, just as Jesus had said it would (Mark 16:7).

How gracious of God: "Tell the disciples *and Peter*." If Peter had not been specifically cited in that announcement, he might not have gone to the empty tomb at all. He was the one who had openly denied Christ. They all did in their own way by their absence, but Peter declared with his own lips and petrified heart, "I don't know him." The message from the women was the pardon of a life sentence. Just when it seemed as if his life was falling into the pit, Christ rescued him and set his feet on an eternal path. Now Peter knew! Christ was alive, Peter was forgiven, and he was indeed destined to be the "rock" on which Christ would build his church. Church history records the ongoing transformation of this man. His sermon at the beginning of the book of Acts reveals a man in love with God and transformed by that love to forgive himself and reach out to a waiting world with the good news of the gospel.

I love the encouragement of the Catholic priest Henri Nouwen in *The Inner Voice of Love:* "Do not despair, thinking that you cannot change yourself after so many years. Simply enter into the presence of Jesus as you are and ask him to give you a fearless heart where he can be with you. *You* cannot make yourself different. *Jesus* came to give you a new heart, a new spirit, a new mind, and a new body. Let him transform you by his love and so enable you to receive his affection in your whole being."

Simply enter into the presence of Jesus.

WHAT A SAVIOR!

I began this project because it seemed to me that we have made Christianity about so much stuff that has nothing to do with loving God. We make it about the version of the Bible we read, which denomination we belong to, what behavior patterns we adhere to, where we send our children to school, what books we read. It's a long, shallow list. Jesus showed us that it's not about following all our little laws; it's about loving God with all our heart, soul, mind, and strength—a short list, the depths of which are fathomless.

There is great liberty in loving God. Let me list just a few of the things we know to be true.

You don't have to fix anyone else's life. God can do that.

You can come to Christ as you are right now. You are loved as you are right now.

God is in control, and he is good.

Your future is secure in him, no matter how things look.

God sees you, he cares for you, and he will shepherd you through uncertain days.

All he asks you to do is to love him.

His love in you makes it possible for you to love others and value yourself as he does.

Christ has left a clear path for you to follow.

God will open the eyes of your heart so you can see Jesus.

You are loved, you are loved, you are loved.

Peter wasn't transformed by getting it all right. In fact it was quite the opposite; Peter got much of it wrong. But through the grace and mercy of God, Peter traded his agenda for Jesus' simple plan. Peter discovered that is all that really matters. I pray each of us, like Peter, will know him, follow him, love him.

> *Jesus, What a Savior*
> You are my strength
> When all my strength has ended.
> You are my hope
> When all my hope is gone.
> You are my joy
> When my world is full of sorrow.
> You're the peace in my tomorrow,
> For I know that you'll be there.
>
> You are my rock
> When I need a place of refuge.

A hand reaching out
When I stumble and I fall.
You are my all
In every time and season.
You are all I've ever needed every time I call.

Jesus, what a Savior you are,
Savior you are.
Jesus, what a Savior you are.

You see the world
With eyes full of compassion.
You feel the hurt
Of the lost and wounded soul.
Little children can know
That your gentle arms will hold them
And you can heal what has been broken.
Take the pain and fill them with hope.

Jesus, what a Savior you are,
Savior you are.
Jesus, what a Savior you are.

You heard our cry.
You answered our plea,
Gave up your life,
Gave us everything.
For all that you are,
Our praises we bring.
We lift up our hearts
And with all of heaven sing.

Jesus, what a Savior you are,
Savior you are.
Jesus, what a Savior you are.
Jesus is all that really matters after all.
　　—Shannon J. Wexelberg

ABOUT THE AUTHOR

Sheila Walsh is a powerful Christian communicator who is a unique combination of author, Bible teacher, speaker, worship leader, and television talk-show host. She is a featured speaker at the nationwide Women of Faith conferences and creator and host of the popular Children of Faith conferences.

The author of the best-selling memoir *Honestly* and more than seventeen other books for adults and children, including *Living Fearlessly, A Love So Big,* and *In Search of the Great White Tiger,* Sheila contributes her wisdom and humor annually to best-selling Women of Faith products coauthored with her conference "Porch Pals": Luci Swindoll, Patsy Clairmont, Marilyn Meberg, Thelma Wells, and Barbara Johnson.

Former co-host of *The 700 Club* and host of her own talk show, *Heart to Heart with Sheila Walsh* on the Family Channel, Sheila is currently working on completing her master's in theology degree from Fuller Seminary. She lives in Nashville, Tennessee, with her husband, Barry, and son, Christian.

Sheila Walsh
ALL THAT REALLY MATTERS
Worship

Drawing upon her Scottish heritage, Sheila Walsh launches listeners towards new depths with God as each lyric communicates the grateful and longing heart of one who truly desires to know Him more. From the dramatic anthem of "A Mighty Fortress Is Our God" to Sheila's passionate rendition of "Here I Am To Worship," Celtic-influenced stylings add a distinct edge to this moving worship album. Available on CD and cassette.

ALBUM IN STORES NOW

AVAILABLE SUMMER 2003

CELTIC LULLABIES & GENTLE WORSHIP

Sheila Walsh combines traditional Celtic instrumentation wrapped in soothing lullabies to create a treasured resource for parents and grandparents alike. Perfect for gift giving.